T0271403

Routledge Revivals

The Relation of Wealth to Welfare

First Published in 1924, *The Relation of Wealth to Welfare* examines certain definite and fundamental elements of human welfare and their relation to private income on the one hand and various kinds of collective action on the other. The four elements discussed in the book are health, art, work, and education. The author argues that the power of private income to increase the welfare of its possessor in regard to the various elements under examination is as a matter of fact frequently or even always comparatively small; whereas the power of collective action and public expenditure to do so is often comparatively great. This book is an essential read for students and researchers of political economy, political studies, and economics in general.

The Relation of Wealth to ...

The Relation of Wealth to Welfare

William A. Robson

Routledge
Taylor & Francis Group

First published in 1924
by George Allen & Unwin Ltd.

This edition first published in 2022 by Routledge
2 Park Square, Milton Park, Abingdon, Oxon, OX14 4RN
and by Routledge
605 Third Avenue, New York, NY 10017

Routledge is an imprint of the Taylor & Francis Group, an informa business

© William A. Robson 1924

Publisher's Note
The publisher has gone to great lengths to ensure the quality of this reprint but
points out that some imperfections in the original copies may be apparent.

Disclaimer
The publisher has made every effort to trace copyright holders and welcomes
correspondence from those they have been unable to contact.

A Library of Congress record exists under LCCN: 25001213

ISBN: 978-1-032-18446-3 (hbk)
ISBN: 978-1-003-25456-0 (ebk)
ISBN: 978-1-032-18447-0 (pbk)

Book DOI 10.4324/9781003254560

THE RELATION OF
WEALTH TO WELFARE

BY

WILLIAM A. ROBSON

LONDON: GEORGE ALLEN & UNWIN LTD.
RUSKIN HOUSE, 40 MUSEUM STREET, W.C. 1

PREFACE

IT is some years ago now since the day when I first realized that the welfare of wealthy persons in regard to quite ordinary matters of everyday life is often very low, and that of poor people relatively high. This obvious fact has, of course, been observed and commented upon by seers and preachers and writers since time immemorial; but the recognition of its truth came to me as a sudden revelation.

When I began to think about the matter I found that the theological explanations which had for centuries been poured out were profoundly unsatisfactory; and I became convinced that the facts which I observed on all hands were due to definite secular causes of a sociological character.

This book is an attempt to describe the economic, psychological and physical nature of some of those causes, and to show the manner in which they operate. It also contains an analysis of certain of the social and personal sources of welfare unconnected with the possession of private income; and an account of the way in which benefits arising from various forms of

5

collective activity, to which but little attention is usually paid, are distributed. Incidentally, I have endeavoured to demonstrate that the subject is capable of being treated in a realistic manner. It is only a beginning, and does not pretend to cover the whole ground.

My best thanks are due to Mrs. Sidney Webb, Mr. J. A. Hobson, and one or two other friends who very kindly read through the manuscript and made several suggestions of great value. Professor Graham Wallas performed a similar service ; but, like everyone else who attended his lectures at the London School of Economics and Political Science, I already owe him so much that a little more can make no difference. From Mr. R. H. Tawney and Sir Henry Slesser I have received much encouragement and useful advice.

W. A. R.

LONDON,
September, 1924.

CONTENTS

FRIDAY, 19*th September*, 1777.

"After breakfast Dr. Johnson and I set out in Dr. Taylor's chaise to go to Derby. The day was fine, and we resolved to go to Keddlestone, the seat of Lord Scarsdale, that I might see his Lordship's fine house. I was struck with the magnificence of the building; and the extensive park, with the finest verdure, covered with deer, and cattle and sheep, delighted me. The number of old oaks, of an immense size, filled me with a sort of respectful admiration : for one of them sixty pounds was offered. The excellent smooth gravel roads; the large piece of water formed by his Lordship from some small brooks, with a handsome barge upon it ; the venerable gothick church, now the family chapel, just by the house; in short, the grand group of objects agitated and extended my mind in a most agreeable manner. 'One should think (said I) that the proprietor of this *must* be happy.' 'Nay, Sir (said Johnson) all this excludes but one evil—poverty.'"

BOSWELL.

"Nor is it strange that latter-day research should confirm so many sayings of the poets. In all great ages art and science have enriched each other."

W. LIPPMAN, *Preface to Politics.*

Monsieur Profond shrugged his shoulders.

"Life's awful like a lot of monkeys scramblin' for empty nuts."

"You're young," said Soames.

If the fellow must make a generalization, he needn't suggest that the forms of property lacked solidity.

JOHN GALSWORTHY, *The Forsyte Saga.*

9

The Relation of Wealth to Welfare

CHAPTER ONE

THE THEME STATED

ONE of the dominant features of the present order of society is the advanced degree to which a system of money economy has taken possession of the minds of men. An attempt is made nowadays to express in terms of money not only the value of all the goods and services of every-day production and exchange, the supply of which normally responds to an increase or decrease in effective demand, but also that of all manner of rare objects or works of art by master craftsmen and creative artists who have long ago gone the way of all flesh, and the supply of whose works therefore remains virtually unaffected by fluctuations in the monetary price.

The conception that the value of an object of human desire can be adequately expressed in terms of money, or the things that money can buy, is not confined to the actual transactions of the marketplace, but has permeated the whole science of economics and the social outlook of large masses of men and women. Professor Pigou, for example, at the commencement of a thousand-page book on economics remarks, "The one obvious instrument of measurement available in social life is money. Hence, the range of our enquiry becomes restricted to that part of social welfare that can be brought directly or indirectly into relation with the measuring rod of money." [1] An instrument of measurement may be obvious without being either adequate or accurate ; and one is reminded of the angler who told a friend that he had no weights with which to weigh the large fish he had caught ; but that it turned the scale against a sack of apples, the kitchen clock and a pair of brown boots.

Professor Marshall, who is commonly regarded throughout the English speaking world as the foremost economist of our time, says in an early chapter of his principal treatise that the money measurement of human motive through its outward manifestations "has made economics more exact than any other branch of social science." [2] The motive on which a man acts " is supplied by a definite amount of money," and it is " this definite and exact money measurement " of certain motives which, according to Dr. Marshall, has enabled economics to rank first among the sciences devoted to the study of man. He warns us on the next

[1] A. C. Pigou, *Economics of Welfare*, p. 11.
[2] A. Marshall, *Principles of Economics*, 8th Ed., p. 14.

12

page that "the economist does not claim to measure any affection of the mind in itself, or directly; but only indirectly through its effect."[1] At the outset, then, Professor Marshall has clearly kept in view the distinction between an "affection of the mind" and an outward effect or action presumed to be the manifestation of that "affection of the mind." It is only the latter, he says, which is capable of measurement in terms of money.

The advantages which this clear separation might have brought to the task of economic analysis are unfortunately lost owing to the fact that Professor Marshall does not maintain the distinction which he had himself drawn between the measurability, in terms of money, of an action or effect and that of a mental state which might or might not be the cause or result of the action. For, he says (to take as a single example a passage which appears twice in the same book), "if the money measure of the happiness caused by two events are equal, there is not in general any very great difference between the amounts of the happiness in the two cases."[2]

Nowhere is this belief in the efficiency of money as a "measuring rod" so prevalent as in the most important of all the subjects of economic enquiry: namely, that relating to the income of individuals and of

---

[1] A. Marshall, *Principles of Economics*, 8th Ed., p. 15.
[2] Ib., p. 131. See also p. 20 for a nearly similar passage.

communities. Professor Marshall says in this con-
nection, " With the growth of a money economy there
has been a strong tendency to confine the notion of
income to those incomings which are in the form of
money." [1] This appears to imply that there are other
incomings [2] which have not been included and which
might conceivably affect the welfare of the person
concerned. But in Professor Marshall's mind there
are apparently no qualifications to his belief that
income and happiness are identical. " When we speak
of the dependence of well-being on material wealth,"
he says, " we refer to the flow or stream of well-being
as measured by the flow or stream of incoming
wealth and the consequent power of using and con-
suming it." In this connexion income must be
distinguished from a capital stock. For although
" a person's stock of wealth yields by its usance and
in other ways an income of happiness . . . there is
little direct connexion between the aggregate amount
of that stock and his aggregate happiness. And *it is
for that reason* that we have throughout this and
preceding chapters spoken of the rich, the middle
classes and the poor as having respectively large,
medium and small incomes—not possessions." [3] In a

[1] A. Marshall, *Principles of Economics*, 8th Ed., p. 71.
[2] In addition to certain payments in kind, such as a free house,
coals, gas, etc., which he includes.
[3] A. Marshall, *Principles of Economics*, 8th Ed. p. 134. The
italics are mine.

later passage, almost at the end of the book, he observes that " It has been assumed that the happiness of life, in so far as it depends on material conditions, may be said to begin when the income is sufficient to yield the *barest* necessaries of life : and after that has been attained, an increase by a given percentage of the income will increase that happiness by about the same amount, whatever the income may be." [1]

Professor Taussig, the leading American economist, adopts the common standpoint, remarking that " for almost all purposes of economic study, it is best to content ourselves with a statement, and an attempt at measurement, in terms not of utility but of money income or real income." [2] The most persistent rebel against this point of view, almost alone among those who have devoted their lives to the serious study of economic science, is Mr. J. A. Hobson. In his book on *Work and Wealth* he points out that this " dominion of the monetary standard is illustrated by the almost instinctive thrill of elation that is felt when we are informed that the income of the nation has risen from about £1,200,000,000 in 1870 to £2,000,000,000 in 1912. So accustomed are we to regard money as the measure of the desirable, that we feel that this rise of money income must imply a corresponding rise in national welfare." [3]

[1] A Marshall, *Principles of Economics*, 8th Ed,, p. 717.   Italics not mine.
[2] F. W. Taussig, *Principles of Economics*, vol. i. p. 134.
[3] J. A. Hobson, *Work and Wealth*, p. 29.

THE RELATION OF WEALTH TO WELFARE

It is of course true that, despite all this talk about money income, no modern economist, nor indeed any one else, any longer confuses wealth with accumulated or flowing masses of gold and silver bullion, as was common enough in Adam Smith's time. Nor is it possible, in an age which has witnessed the unique spectacle of half the currencies of Europe becoming inflated to an almost fantastic degree, for anyone to regard what formerly used to be understood by money income as being necessarily identical with the nominal amount of currency now received by a person by way of income. It is now plain to the stupidest intelligence that a rising money income has in many places and at many times in the world that followed the outbreak of the great war of 1914 been accompanied by a decrease in the amount of commodities and services which a given unit of that income could command. And in consequence of this the phrases " real wages " and " real income " have passed from the textbooks of the economists, where they had long reposed in a comfortable obscurity, into the everyday language of plain men and women. But all that is denoted by these phrases is an endeavour to get behind the fluctuating uncertainties to which all existing forms of money are subject, and to reckon a man's income in terms of what Irving Fisher calls the " market basket " of commodities which a unit of it can at a given moment purchase. The word " real " in this connexion has

16

no other meaning, either ethical or social, religious or philosophical ; and the standard by which variations in real income are tested is usually an index number calculated from the prices current at a given date of food, textiles, coal, house accommodation and other articles of widespread consumption. All that has happened, in fact, is that the conception of income has been shifted to some extent from money to the things which the individual can purchase therewith ; and when Professor Patrick Geddes, the authority on Town Planning, remarks that " From the smallest Labour Union to the greatest Banking Trust, all are hypnotized, from their earliest education with its exaggeration of money arithmetic, into a specialized insistence upon money gains, which practically amounts to a veritable obsession by these, with consequent practical blindness to real wealth for themselves and to real wages for others,"[1] he is using the words " real wealth " and " real wages " in quite a different sense to that in which they are employed nowadays by economists and those who follow their use of words.

It is no exaggeration to say that the most important assumption underlying the capitalist system is the belief that human welfare, if not happiness, is closely correlated to money income or real income. For although, as Dr. Cannan remarks, " it is a commonplace now . . . that material welfare does not increase *pari*

---

[1] Patrick Geddes, *Cities in Evolution*, p. 68.

B

passu with increasing income," [1] it is a commonplace for the most part only among economists ; and production and distribution under capitalist conditions depend mainly on the notion that a man's well-being will increase as his income increases. For unless the income of a man is regarded as an index to his material welfare, it becomes clear that the desire for a larger income cannot be relied upon as an adequate motive for the production of wealth, since what men and women really seek through their economic activities is not income but welfare. At that point the bottom would fall out of the argument that the motive of profit-making is not only sufficient but indispensable for maintaining production, because no man is fool enough to strive for an increase of income unless he believes that it will bring him a proportionate, or nearly proportionate, increase of well-being.

Although they have never ventured to attempt an evaluation of the economic welfare of human beings except in terms of money, or of the goods and services that can be brought into relation with " the measuring rod of money," there is to be observed in the writings of the most prominent economists a distinct note of uneasiness as to the efficacy of this method of treating the subject which has hitherto prevailed. " There is no guarantee," says Professor Pigou, " that the effects produced on the part of welfare

---

[1] E. Cannan, *The Economic Outlook*, p. 273.

that can be brought into relation with the measuring
rod of money may not be cancelled by effects of a
contrary kind brought about in other parts, or aspects,
of welfare : and, if this happens, *the practical usefulness
of our conclusions is wholly destroyed.*" [1]   Could mis-
giving go farther ? " The spirit of the age," writes
Marshall, " induces a closer attention to the question
whether our increasing wealth may not be made to go
farther than it does in promoting the general well-
being ; and this again compels us to examine how far
the exchange value of any element of wealth, whether
in collective or individual use, represents accurately
the addition which it makes to happiness and well-
being." [2]

Despite the admission that what Marshall calls
" the spirit of the age " compels us to examine the
relation between the exchange value of an object of
human desire and its contribution to human welfare,
no economist, with the honourable exception of Mr.
Hobson, has ever made a serious attempt to do so.
And for fairly clear reasons. With the progressive
development during the past hundred and fifty years
of the old political economy into the modern subject of
economics, the whole tendency has been for economic
discussion to become in the first place increasingly
preoccupied with the more easily measurable facts of
human nature and lamentably anxious to avoid those

[1] Op. cit., p. 12.   The italics are mine.   [2] Op. cit., p. 85.

presenting greater difficulty ; in the second place to call in the aid of the pure and natural sciences of mathematics, statistics, and biology ; and in the third place to become detached from all questions of political morality or human value. Thus, curiously enough, the divorce between contemporary economics and contemporary psychology, though both are now independent sciences, and sprung from a common parentage, is greater than that which existed at almost any other time in their history, despite the efforts of Mr. Graham Wallas and one or two other social psychologists to bridge the gulf. Hence, although Ruskin pointed out generations ago that " political economy, being a science of wealth, must be a science respecting human capacities and dispositions " ; [1] and although Mr. Pigou, professor of political economy in the University of Cambridge, in our own day confesses that " welfare consists of states of consciousness only and not material things," [2] we have not got much farther with the investigation into the relation between economic goods and those " states of consciousness." Nor are we likely to do so as long as the economist " does not attempt to weigh the real value of the higher affections against those of our lower," nor " balance the love for virtue against the desire for agreeable food." [3]

Nearly a decade ago Mr. Wallas tried to project

[1] J. Ruskin, *Unto this Last*, p. 111, Cassell's Ed.
[2] Op. cit., p. 10.
[3] Marshall, op. cit., p. 16.

the discussion on to another plane ; and in doing so pointed out certain truths which no one had previously noticed. " The most important effects of a diminution of the happiness of a whole class," he wrote, " take long to reveal themselves, and cannot easily be balanced against an increase in wages." [1] But no one took up the thread ; and although economists have enlarged their conception of the nature of material welfare to a considerable extent since the middle of last century, economics remains non-moral and non-psychological in the criteria which it applies to wealth.

Laissez faire individualism, we have seen, holds out as a dominant attraction to its votaries the possibility of obtaining a large private income. The modern student of social thought, no less than the private observer of human nature, is led to enquire, quite apart from all Socialist contentions regarding the inexpediency or immorality of large inequalities of wealth, and regardless of expert economic arguments concerning the marginal utility of income, whether and to what extent a private income, however large, necessarily includes many of the essential elements of the good life or the happy life. Such an investigation is the purpose of this book. Can we agree comfortably with Dr. Marshall when he says that " as money is likely to be turned to the higher uses of life in about equal proportions, by any two large groups of people

[1] Graham Wallas, *The Great Society*, p. 350.

taken without special bias from any two parts of the western world, there is even some *primâ facie* probability that equal additions to their material resources will make about equal additions to the fulness of life, and the true progress of the human race " ; [1] or must we share Mr. Hobson's scepticism when he remarks that "even the general assumption that every growth of wealth enhances welfare cannot be admitted without qualification ? " [2]

If we find that private income does not yield to its possessor all or some of the most essential elements of welfare, in what other quarter should we seek them ? One source that may be suggested is public expenditure and collective action by the community as a whole, considered not as mere potential forms of associated effort existing in the ideal programmes of social reformers, but regarded more definitely in the light of the contribution which they actually make to the life of the individual under present conditions. No form of human co-operation has been so sedulously ignored, misrepresented, underrated and discredited, save in the one ·ghastly province where its effects are hideous and destructive. None is more deserving of impartial analysis.

It is nearly three-quarters of a century ago since Herbert Spencer wrote that " not only does a govern-

[1] Marshall, *Principles*, p. 20.
[2] Hobson, *Work and Wealth*, p. 5.

22

ment reverse its function by taking away more property than is needed for protective purposes, but even what it gives, in return for the excess so taken, is in essence a loss." [1] Recent events in post-war England have shown, however, that, except for the addition of the payment of interest to bondholders to their former conception of the single legitimate function of the State, the majority of the large property-owners and captains of industry are still to a large extent Spencerian in their views as to the legitimate objects of public expenditure. The wild cries for " more production," unqualified by any other consideration, which have rent the air during the past few years, appear to indicate that the economic outlook of the wealthier classes dates to a period even prior to Herbert Spencer ; and it is only here and there that a great employer has had the quality of mind to desert the shadow and grasp the substance in the manner of Henry Ford who, rich beyond the dreams of avarice, can yet say " we are too wrapped up in the things we are doing—we are not enough concerned with the reasons why we do them. Our whole competitive system, our whole ·creative expression, all the play of our faculties seem to be centred around material production and its by-products of success and wealth." [2] John Ruskin had already said much the same thing with his " There is no wealth

[1] Herbert Spencer, *Social Statics*, Last Ed., p. 68.
[2] Henry Ford, *My Life and Work*, p. 274.

but life," but no sensible person could be expected to pay a cranky art critic the same attention as that commanded by a great industrialist such as Henry Ford, with his untold billions, his five thousand cars a day, and his lack of culture.

However this may be, it is my intention to examine one by one certain definite elements in human welfare, and to consider separately the effects in the life of the individual of private income on the one hand and of collective action and public expenditure on the other hand. On all questions of ultimate value it is impossible not to be to some extent controversial; but I shall discuss only those elements which are likely by common consent to be generally admitted as necessary to the good life of man upon earth. But first let me suggest that quite apart from any preconceived theories concerning the relative advantages of individual effort and collective action, everyone must agree with Professor Hobhouse, the sociologist, when he says that "Of collective achievement as of collective aims, it holds good that its value is to be tested by its bearing on the actual lives of men and women." [1] It may be true that, as another writer remarks, " to reform our notions of what is valuable and distinguished would bring about an economic reformation "; [2] but to-day most people who are seriously interested in the progres-

[1] L. T. Hobhouse, *The Elements of Social Justice*, p. 30.
[2] Vernon Lee, *Laurus Nobilis*, p. 70.

24

THE THEME STATED

sive development of society feel that it is futile to pay
attention to what would happen if our notions were
different from what they in fact are, until we have
discovered what actually happens with human nature
in its present state. My investigations will therefore
tend to be realistic rather than speculative, inasmuch
as they will be concerned with actual events and possible
changes arising out of existing conditions. Realism in
this sense is in no way opposed either to ideals or to
idealism, except insofar as those ideals refuse to face
the facts of human nature here and now, and postulate
the eradication of man's present imperfections by a
process undescribed and unexplained.

VARIATIONS ON THE THEME

CHAPTER TWO

HEALTH

IT will be generally admitted that physical health is for every man and woman an essential condition of well-being, and it is for this reason that. it will receive our first consideration as an element of welfare.

The relation between private wealth and personal health is by no means a simple one, once we get above the line of extreme poverty. When we leave out the classes which live no considerable distance above the level of mere subsistence, and whose deaths from an insufficiency of food, clothing, warmth and house accommodation swell the death-rate and the infant mortality rate, there is but little evidence to show that increased income leads to better personal health. Even in the case of the diseases which are definitely attributable to a pecuniary inability to purchase the commodities necessary for the preservation of health, it would appear that immunity is reached by the addition of a very small increase of income. Rickets is a typical example of a disease due in many cases to poverty, and is largely caused by a lack of the vitamins contained in milk.[1] But the following table, which is an analysis of the weekly income of the families of two hundred children, shows that a difference of only a few shillings a week in the family income may be sufficient to avert the disease.

Condition.	Weekly Income.		
	No. 1–100.	No. 101–200.	Average of 200.
	s. d.	s. d.	s. d.
Markedly rachitic ..	28 3½	32 7½	30 5½
Slightly rachitic ..	31 1	33 0	32 0½
Non-rachitic	31 1	38 10¼	35 0

Thus it may be observed that " although there was a difference of about 15 per cent. in the average family income between the markedly rachitic and the non-rachitic groups, they belonged to the same social class." [2] It appears from this and other evidence that there is no relationship at all between rickets and income when the latter exceeds about forty shillings a week. This is only another way of saying that the marginal utility of income falls rapidly so far as rickets

[1] *The Hygiene of Food and Drink*, published by Board of Education, 1921, p. 9.
[2] *Social and Economic Factors [in the Causation of Rickets*, p. 75. Medical Research Committee. Special Report Series, No. 20/1918.

is concerned.[1] This may be true of health in all its phases; and if we classified the whole nation into definite categories of physical health on a scientific quantitative basis, instead of merely distinguishing the living, the sick and the dead, it is easily conceivable that an actual falling off of health might be shown to exist among certain classes after a fairly high point on the ascending scale of incomes had been reached. For many of the habits of life customary among persons with large incomes, such as the eating of excessive quantities of highly-seasoned food,[2] late hours, the living in an atmosphere of continuous excitement, and a general irregularity of existence, are as destructive of health at one end of the scale as, at the other end, are the lack of proper nourishment, overwork, monotony, and the insanitary overcrowding which victimize the poorer and more helpless members of the community.

" In England, owing to prosperity, over-eating has

[1] Or that the coefficient of correlation between rickets and income approaches zero when income reaches about 40s. per week. Cf. *Rickets. The Relative Importance of Environment and Diet as Factors in Causation* (Medical Research Council. Special Report Series, No. 68/1922), *passim*, which points to the same conclusion.

[2] " Many people suppose that expensive foods are more nutritious than cheaper ones, and will stint themselves to provide these supposed delicacies for weakly children. In point of fact many of such expensive foods (e.g. oysters, asparagus, caviare, etc.) are physiologically inferior to those costing much less; some of them possess hardly any nutritive value at all. The value of a food should by no means be measured by its cost or tastiness. The golden rule of dietary is temperance in quantity, plainness in quality."—*The Hygiene of Food and Drink*, Board of Education, 1921, p. 18.

28

become habitual with many," writes Mr. Leonard Hill, F.R.S., in one of the most interesting of the official reports of the Medical Research Council.[1] " A young man, poor, keen, active and frugal, when he gets prosperous will overload his stomach three or four times a day. . . . The natural inclination of man, when well-to-do and engaged in sedentary occupation, is to raise his metabolism rate by increasing the protein value of the diet. He takes also alcohol, or hot stimulating drinks, and thus replaces the natural increase of metabolism and warmth of skin which is produced by open-air exercise. . . . The overfed man of means takes rides in fast motor-cars and thus secures a high cooling power to relieve him of the heat generated by his meat and drink. Thus uselessly and most uneconomically is the energy of food and petrol wasted on the self-indulgent."

In a later passage Mr. Hill points out that " children of the well-to-do are kept indoors for fear of catching cold . . . and are often wrongly fed or over-indulged. They may suffer from the conditions of environment . . . no less, and perhaps even more, than children of the poor who play in the streets."[2]

During the war of 1914–1918 an elaborate survey was actually made of a large section of the adult male population of Great Britain, the health and physique

[1] *The Science of Ventilation and Open Air Treatment*, Part II (Medical Research Council. Special Report Series, No. 52/1920), p. 114. [2] Ib., p. 196.

of which were determined on a quantitative basis by the Ministry of National Service acting through its Medical Boards. The results of this remarkable investigation, unique in the history of the nation, are of the greatest interest to our discussion.

Between 1st November, 1917, and 31st October, 1918, no less than 2,425,184 medical examinations were made of men of military age. Every man who was thus examined was placed in one or another of four distinct medical categories. Grade I consisted of those who had attained the full normal standard of health and strength, and who were capable of enduring physical exertion suitable to their age.[1] Such men must not have been suffering from progressive organic disease, nor have any serious disability or deformity. Minor defects capable of being remedied or adequately compensated by artificial means were not regarded as disqualifications. Grade II took in all those who for various causes, such as partial disability, could not reach the standard of Grade I, but whose physical condition was too high for Grades III or IV. Men in Grade II were not to suffer from progressive organic disease ; must have fair hearing and vision ; be of moderate muscular development, and be able to undergo a considerable degree of physical exertion of a nature not involving severe strain. Grade III consisted of all

[1] It appears that the accuracy of the results was therefore not affected by differences in age.

men who presented marked physical disabilities, or who gave such evidence of past disease as not to be considered fit to undergo the degree of physical exertion required for the higher grades. This third Grade included those who were fit only for clerical or other sedentary occupations, such as tailoring and boot-making. The lowest Grade, No. IV, comprised all men who were totally and permanently unfit for any form of military service.[1]

Something will be said later regarding the general results arrived at from this great survey of the physical condition of the nation. What we are immediately concerned with here are certain data obtained from specific portions of the survey. In the London Region, for example, the health grading of 160,545 men was tabulated, according to their occupation group, as shown on pp. 32–3.[2]

In the following Table the groups have been arranged in a descending scale according to the percentages in Grade I. Grade I, it will be recalled, consists of thoroughly healthy and physically perfect men ; and men in Grade II may also be regarded as being healthy and fit rather than the contrary. The final column on the right-hand side (Column A) consists of the percentages in Grades I and II added together ; and represents therefore approximately the percentage of

[1] *Ministry of National Service Report upon Physical Examination of Men of Military Age, etc.*, Cmd. 504/1920, vol. i. p. 42.
[2] Ib., Chart I.

OCCUPATION.	GRADES. (Per cent. of men in each.)				Column A. I and II added together.
	I.	II.	III.	IV.	
1. AGRICULTURE .. .. including farmer servants, gardeners, foresters, game-keepers, golf professionals, caddies, etc.	38	21	30	11	59
2. SKILLED ARTISANS .. .. including munition workers, of all kinds, aeroplane constructors, plumbers, gas fitters, carpenters, engineers, painters, blacksmiths, etc.	37	25	29	9	62
3. SEAMEN .. .. including fishermen, lightermen, etc.	36	14	41	9	50
4. TRANSPORT .. .. including outdoor porters, messengers, taxi-drivers, bus drivers, conductors, tram drivers, carters, draymen, postmen, railway servants and porters (other than clerks), etc.	31	21	36	12	52

32

5. LABOUR .. .. including unskilled labourers, scavengers, dockers, etc.	47	14	39	21	26
6. INDOOR (SEDENTARY) .. .. .. including clerks, piece-workers (cloth trade), tailors, bootmakers, printers and compositors, etc.	49	12	39	23	26
7. INDOOR (ACTIVE).. .. .. .. including hotel servants and porters, indoor servants (except waiters and chefs), shop-keepers and assistants (except those concerned with food), teachers, legal profession, dental profession and dental mechanics, chemists, etc.	49	13	38	26	23
8. TRADESMEN .. .. including shopkeepers and assistants concerned with food, milkmen, waiters, chefs, etc.	41	13	46	23	18
9. BARBERS .. .. including complexion specialists, chiropodists, bone-setters, manicurists, masseurs, Turkish bath attendants.	33	21	46	17	16

33

C

the men in each occupation group who are not definitely unhealthy or suffering from physical disability or under-development. The addition of the first two grades results, as shown in this column, in a slight shifting of the physical 'order of merit' of the occupation groups, but there is no fundamental change to be observed save that Group 5 (Labour) drops down two places to seventh in the list.

The significance of the statistics which we have reproduced lies in the fact that they demonstrate conclusively the absence of a direct relationship between private income and personal health, even when large groups are examined. Agriculture is one of the worst paid occupations in England, yet those who work at it form the healthiest (or second healthiest, if Column A be taken) section in the nation. The average income of the members of the Indoor (Active) Group is almost certainly higher than that of any other in the list, including as it does the highly paid legal and dental professions, the teachers and the chemists ; yet the relatively great personal wealth of these men does not secure for them a passable standard of health and fitness, and the group ranks seventh in the list as regards Grade I and sixth if Grades I and II are taken together. The earnings of seamen are considerably lower than those of the tradesmen in Group 8, but the seamen are far healthier than the waiters and chefs and shopkeepers.

HEALTH

It may be remarked that the expert Committee which drafted the report took into consideration the possibility of each occupation acting as a kind of selective agent on a physical basis upon those who were attracted to it. But after careful investigation this simple explanation was rejected. " It can hardly be doubted," the Committee observe, " that the gradual fall in the index of fitness . . . is a true criterion of the various occupations upon the physical welfare of the workers. They correspond to what we know of the conditions of life in several trades and their accepted effect upon health too closely to be explained by the hypothesis that the agriculturist is an agriculturist because he is healthy, and the tailor a tailor because he is unhealthy." [1]

Even more striking is a table giving the incidence of tuberculosis of the lungs according to occupation among 895 recruits examined at Liverpool, representing a characteristic cross-section of the male inhabitants of that city. There, among nearly 150 specified occupations, we find *seriatim* clerks 109, managers 51, carters 38. . . . Yet the income of " managers " must obviously be enormously greater than that of carters. Again, there were five more cases of consumption among " salesmen " than among " dock labourers," though the earnings of salesmen

[1] *Ministry of National Service Report upon Physical Examination of Men of Military Age, etc.*, Cmd, 504/1920. vol. i. p. 18.

are considerably larger than those of dockers. Porters and engineers, dentists and packers, shipowner and newsvendor jostle one another in the list giving the incidence of the dread disease among their categories ; [1] and ever and again the disparity of income betokens the failure of private wealth to purchase health. The money wages of metal workers are higher than those of pastoral workers ; but the physique of the metal worker is poor, while shepherds are "splendidly developed and usually sound." [2] In Manchester the medical experts of the Ministry of National Service discovered that the most fertile cause of poor physique in children is " not due to poverty (except in a practically negligible number of cases) but to the lack of knowledge of the mothers (who could have afforded to buy the necessary food) as to how to cook it." [3] There is no evidence to show that a knowledge of the hygienic and physiological principles of child nurture increases, any more than the health of the adult, with increases of private income ; and it was no doubt a recognition of this which led those responsible for the official report to recommend public instruction in those principles as " the scientific method of dealing with the question of ' Poor Physique.' "

[1] *Ministry of National Service Report upon Physical Examination of Men of Military Age, etc.*, Cmd. 504/920, vol. i. p. 45. See also the Table showing the military classification of 1,000 each of " Middle Class Men," Clerks, Craftsmen and Open Air Workers in London and South-Eastern Region, p. 36.
[2] Ib., p. 17.   [3] Ib., p. 43.

HEALTH

Some very interesting new evidence has recently been brought to light as a result of scientific investigation into the conditions regulating child life. The remarkable fact has been established that " the normal average birth weight and length are fully maintained despite varying maternal circumstances "[1] of an economic character. Carefully tabulated measurements show that " if there is any correlation between income and birth-weight or income and length at birth it is in any case exceedingly small and of no practical importance " ;[2] and the existence of any correlation at all is " very doubtful." Dr. John Brownlee, in an enquiry of a different character, remarks that the child before it is born is " protected against the vicissitudes of the mother and more or less independent even of her starvation or dissipation."[3] At the same time, " there is a group of diseases which apparently kill quite independently of the environment of the child or the mother."[4]

The main point to be noticed, however, and one which is illustrated by the survey of the Ministry of National Service to which reference has been made above, is the fact that for the most part both rich and

[1] *Child Life Investigations : The Effect of Maternal Social Conditions and Nutrition upon Birth Weight and Length* (Medical Research Council. Special Report, Series No. 81/1924), p. 30.
[2] Ib., p. 18.
[3] *The Use of Death Rates as a Measure of Hygienic Conditions* (Medical Research Council. Special Report, Series No. 60/1922), p. 27. [4] Loc. cit.

poor pass the greater part of their waking lives in an environment which, so far as hygiene is concerned, is to a large extent a common one, particularly in the great urban areas ; and they are therefore subject to approximately similar conditions of health, regardless of differences in income. Nearly two hundred tons of impurity hang suspended in the air over London at 10 a.m. on a foggy morning,[1] and " there is a tendency noticeable for the death rate to have a maximum when the impurity is highest, or rather a little later than the maximum impurity." [2] Both the atomized impurity and the shadow of death hang over rich and poor alike, and care nought for the inequalities of wealth which count for so much in the eyes of the world below.

A captain of industry in Lombard Street with an income of twenty thousand pounds a year will do most of his work under almost the same physical conditions as one of his junior clerks earning two pounds a week. He will have a larger and more luxurious office, it is true, but he will be subject to the same absence of fresh air, the same loss of physical exuberance through sedentary work as his obscure acolyte. And although he will drive home in a sumptuous limousine instead of fighting his way into a train or motorbus or tramcar he may suffer even more acutely from lack of exercise than his employee who has faced the nightly Armageddon of the privately-owned traffic system or who

[1] Report of Advisory Committee on Atmospheric Pollution. M.O. 249/1922, p. 26.   [2] Ib., p. 6.

has walked a few miles on the homeward path to save expense. And when he dies, his lungs will be as black from London smoke as those of any other city dweller.

The hygienic conditions of life in our great cities are, indeed, in so many ways common to all who work in them, irrespective of income, that unless the wealthy employer is willing to remove himself into an entirely different environment, and thereby probably cut himself off from most of the things that lend flavour and interest and zest to his life, all his thousands can secure for him only the most trifling additions to personal health, and scarcely none which are not available to any workman or clerk who takes the trouble to investigate the basic requirements of health.

The Chief Medical Officer of Health has remarked that " the sound foundation of personal and national health is the body of man " [1]—not his income. During the nineteenth century the problem of public health was thought to depend almost entirely upon the attainment of external environmental cleanliness, such as a pure water supply, good sanitation and so forth. To-day, the ablest exponents of public health have come to attach considerable importance to personal hygiene, which may be regarded as the attainment of cleanliness inside the body. " For the maintenance of vigorous health the disciplined exercise of the

[1] *On the State of the Public Health* (Annual Report of the Chief Medical Officer of the Ministry of Health), 1921, p. 21.

39

body in the open air for some period of the day is of very great importance," [1] observes Mr. Leonard Hill, F.R.S., and he suggests a six-mile walk or work of an equivalent amount on an allotment as a suitable form. Exercise and fresh air, moderation in eating and drinking, a careful regard for dietetic principles in the choice of food, clothing of a texture which does not overheat the body and impede the metabolic processes—these are the requirements of good health on which chief stress is laid by the most distinguished authorities on personal hygiene of the present day.[2] But not one of these requirements makes excessive demands on the private income of an individual, or is outside the reach of the slender purse of even the great mass of weekly wage-earners. The evidence, in fact, is nearly all the other way, and goes to show that the wealthier classes have a strong tendency to those forms of self-indulgence which are most opposed to the principles of personal hygiene on which health depends. In 150 cases of very long-lived persons analysed by Sir Herman Weber [3] the great majority consisted of temperate, small meat-eaters who lived much in the open air,

[1] *The Science of Ventilation and Open Air Treatment*, Part I (Medical Research Committee. Special Report, Series No. 32/1919), p. 77.

[2] Ib., p. 77. See also the following Special Reports of the Medical Research Council : No. 73/1923, *Studies of Body Heat and Efficiency* ; No. 38/1924, *Report on the Present State of Knowledge of Accessory Food Factors (Vitamins)* " ; No. 52/1920, *Science of Ventilation and Open Air Treatment*, Part II.

[3] *Longevity and Prolongation of Life*, 5th Ed., 1919.

and led an active life full of work. Many of them had a life of toil with great restrictions as to their food and comforts. Only a few were self-indulgent or intemperate, or idle and lazy persons.

It would appear, therefore, that so far as personal hygiene is concerned, it is wrong to assume that an improvement is likely to be brought about in the life of the individual by increases of private income. The only effective method undoubtedly appears to be that of systematic education in the principles of hygiene; and it is obvious that this could not be carried out on a large scale save by collective enterprise.

Most of the conditions of personal health are, in fact, more dependent upon public control than upon private income, once a minimum of decency has been secured by the latter (a qualification not to be overlooked); and this is especially true if we regard health not as something negative acquired by the process of recovering from disease, but, in the light of the modern doctrine of preventive medicine, as a condition of positive immunity not merely from illness but from the deteriorating effects of the physical evils arising from civilized life as we know it to-day. It is true that the wealthier classes are able to afford expensive medical advice and costly treatment inaccessible to the poor even through the medium of a hospital; and in certain cases they may derive benefit therefrom. But the advantage is somewhat exceptional, and one which in the main affects only people whose health has already become seriously impaired. The absence of financial worry has a certain value in relation to health ; and it might be thought that the richer people became the more their health would be likely to benefit on this account. But a careful observation of human nature indicates that the habit of worrying over monetary matters arises more from an inherent disposition to do so than from an absolute objective cause ; and freedom from financial care is by no means the rule or even common among well-to-do people. Again, with the eight-hour day almost universally in operation in England the differential advantage from the point of view of health previously enjoyed by the better-off classes, who alone had adequate opportunities for leisure and rest, has largely disappeared. It might conceivably be argued that a person with an income of £50 a year could become twice as healthy with an income of £100 ; but it is obvious that a man earning £700 a year will not be enabled, by an increase of £70 per annum, either to become a ten per cent. healthier individual or to extend the length of his life by one-tenth of its span. Examples of this kind enable us to see how rapidly decreasing is the marginal utility of income so far as health is concerned. But fundamentally all such attempts at correlation are meaningless without a quantitative calculus of bodily health, except in so far as they illustrate the extent to which the element of health lies outside the sphere of private purchase.

It is the inability of the individual to control the hygienic conditions of the common environment that has made collective effort in this province of such enormous value in the lives of the men, women and children who comprise the nation.

In 1850 Herbert Spencer declared that " this doctrine, that it is the duty of the State to protect the health of its subjects, cannot be established, for the same reason that its kindred doctrines cannot, namely, the impossibility of saying how far the alleged duty shall be carried." [1] All the " impatiently agitated schemes for improving our sanitary conditions by Act of Parliament were," he said, " needless, inasmuch as there are already efficient influences at work gradually accomplishing every desideratum." [2] But Spencer's opposition to public health was based, not so much on the belief that individual enterprise would succeed in preventing or securing immunity from the disastrous outbreaks of cholera and typhus which wrought frequent havoc in England throughout the first half of the nineteenth century, as on the principle that it would be better to perish in agony rather than to accept assistance from the community in its collective aspect. For, said he, " even could State agency

[1] *Social Statics*, by H. Spencer, Final Ed., pp. 105–6.
[2] Ib., p. 108.

compass for our towns the most perfect salubrity, it would in the end be better to remain as we are rather than to obtain such a benefit by such means." [1] The levying of rates and taxes for such a purpose was, in his view, an act of aggression on the part of the State.[2]

Nearly three-quarters of a century have passed since Spencer tried to strangle the first tentative efforts of the pioneers of English sanitary reform, and it is now possible to see what have been the broad results of that movement. In 1850, when Spencer published his *Social Statics*, the general death rate for England and Wales was 19·9, and the infantile mortality per 1,000 births was 146.[3] The decrease in the death rates since then is shown by the following table : [4]

	Average Annual Death Rate per 1,000 Living.	Average Annual Infant Mortality (i.e. Deaths of Children under one Year per 1,000 Births.)
1871–80	21·4	149
1881–90	19·1	142
1891–1900	18·2	153
1900–1910	15·4	128
1911–1920	14·3	100
1920	12·4	80
1921	12·1	83
1922	12·8	77

[1] *Social Statics*, by H. Spencer, Final Ed., p. 112. [2] Ib., p. 114.
[3] *Public Health Administration*, by B. G. Bannington, p. 323.
[4] Annual Report of the Chief Medical Officer of the Ministry of Health, 1922, p. 7. The figures include civilian mortality only from 1915–1918.

HEALTH

" Previously to the nineties of last century," says the Chief Medical Officer in a recent report, " the decline (in the death rate) apart from infant mortality, chiefly affected the lower ages, but recently there has been apparent an improvement in the middle years of life." [1] The reason for this may be found by examining the statistics of some of the principal infectious diseases.[2]

	1871–1880.		1911–1920.	
	Number of Deaths.	Death Rate per 1,000 Population.	Number of Deaths.	Death Rate per 1,000 Population.
Smallpox	5,742	0·24	14	0·000
Enteric fever.. ..	7,842	0·32	1,278	0·03 5
Scarlet fever	17,423	0·72	1,706	0·047
Tuberculosis (pulmonary)..	51,510	2·13	38,775	1·079
Tuberculosis (other than pulmonary) ..	18,248	0·75	12,621	0·351
Typhus fever.. ..	1,398	0·06	5	0·000
Whooping cough ..	12,453	0·51	6,538	0·184

What has occurred, broadly speaking, during the past seventy years, is that " typhus and cholera have been practically wiped out, smallpox, despite the increase of unvaccinated persons, has been reduced to small and easily-controlled proportions, typhoid fever

[1] Annual Report of the Chief Medical Officer of the Ministry of Health, 1922, p. 28. One cause of this is the reduction of maternal mortality from 4,455 deaths in 1900 (4·81 per cent.) to 2,971 in 1922 (3·71 per cent.). [2] Bannington, op. cit., p. 24.

has been diminished by four-fifths, and deaths from tuberculosis have undergone a fifty per cent reduction."[1] These results have been due almost entirely to the work of the public medical service,[2] as anyone can discover by studying the elaborate reports issued annually by the Ministry of Health (or its predecessor the Local Government Board) and the local Medical Officers of Health.

Yet even such an enthusiast as Mr. B. G. Bannington can be so blind to the nature of the work in which he is professionally engaged as to remark that "From the financial point of view one fact about the public health department stands out prominently; it is essentially a spending, not an earning department."[3] It is one thing to say that the distributed benefits derived from the sanitary and medical activities undertaken by the community in its collective aspect, which we call public health, do not enter into the private income, as calculated in terms of money, of the persons who share in the dividend. It is quite another to say

[1] Bannington, op. cit., p. 323.

[2] The records of separate areas, and the methods adopted, may often be found in the reports of local Medical Officers of Health, and in special studies on the subject. See, for example, *Sanitation in Paisley, a Record of Progress*, by W. W. Kelso (1922). Mr. Kelso shows that the average death rate in Paisley was reduced from 26·52 per 1,000 in 1855 to 13·80 in 1920; that deaths from scarlet fever fell from 77 in 1883 to nothing in 1917, though over a hundred cases were notified in that year; that deaths from smallpox and typhus fever have been eliminated, and that enteric is practically a thing of the past. See pp. 389 et seq.

[3] B. G. Bannington, *Public Health Administration*, p. 253.

46

that the public health service is a spending or con-
suming department, as contrasted with those that
" earn." The public medical service spends, it is
true, nearly seven million pounds a year in preventing
disease [1] (excluding expenditure on National Health
Insurance), but it earns very large " dividends " in
terms, not of money, but of health. The distribution
of these " dividends " or " profits " takes place, not
through the medium of money, but in kind. Rich
and poor share alike in the benefits, and no attempt
is made by a citizen to estimate in terms of money the
immunity from cholera or typhus which has been
secured to him during the preceding year by the
drainage system constructed and maintained by the
Public Health Department of his municipality ; or to
evaluate in pounds, shillings and pence the services
rendered to him and his family by the sanitary
inspectors during, let us say, the year 1922, when
7,106 cases of adulterated or injurious food were discovered among 113,860 samples purchased for analysis.[2]
Among the samples analysed were lemonade containing
tartaric acid ; jam containing dyes and salicylic acids ;
cocoa containing arsenic ; and aerated waters con-
taminated with copper, lead or zinc.

[1] See Public Social Services (Total expenditure under certain
Acts of Parliament), 139, 1922, p. 5.
[2] Fourth Annual Report of the Ministry of Health Cmd 1944/1923,
p. 23 et seq. See also Annual Report of the Government Chemist
upon the work of the Government Laboratory.

THE RELATION OF WEALTH TO WELFARE

" In a true sense the nation can buy health," says Sir George Newman, the Chief Medical Officer of Health, in a striking passage ; [1] but only, we should add, in its collective capacity, so far as many of the first, essentials of hygiene are concerned. The mid-Victorian era was far more reluctant to engage in collective enterprise than is the generation of our own day ; and if health could have been purchased by the individual out of his private income, there would be no public health service to-day. But it could not be so purchased ; and nowadays we can see that more and more of the environmental conditions upon which health depends must come within the province of public control if the physical well-being of the indivi-dual, rich or poor, is to be assured. It is becoming increasingly clear that there is almost no such thing as

[1] The passage is as follows : " In a true sense the nation can buy health, but the ' goods ' are not delivered on the date of payment. Public expenditure on national health is like expenditure on a lifeboat or a fire engine ; even more, it is like a long term invest-ment. It yields its interest with absolute certainty, a thousand-fold, but only in the course of years and sometimes in the course of generations. It is money hidden in maternity, in good schools, in pure food, in clean streets, in sanitary houses, in an abundant water supply, in dispensaries, hospitals and sanitoria, and in the vast network of a sanitary and protective cordon in every village and city in the land. . . .

" Sometimes we hear the idle question, What is the use of all our expenditure on health ? It is often asked by persons who do not reflect that their welcome presence among us, alive, alert, and competent, is itself the answer."—Annual Report of the Chief Medical Officer of the Ministry of Health, 1921, p. 9. *On the State of the Public Health.*

private health. All health is public in the sense that it is a matter of public concern, though not necessarily within the realm of the public medical service. If we care whether a woman dies of puerperal fever in child-birth, we must also care whether her husband is unable to work efficiently because he suffers from headaches. But although we attempt to prevent the puerperal fever through the activities of the local medical officer of health and his staff, we may nevertheless leave the man to manage his own headache as best he can, unless it becomes plain that the headache, like the puerperal fever, is an affair largely beyond the control of the individual and his income, and one which can be more effectively dealt with by the community in its collective aspect.

One of the environmental causes which bring about not only headaches, but many other far more serious disabilities, is the excessive noise which is the special characteristic of modern industrial and city life, and which, in the words of a well-known psychologist, is a "factor causing wastage of energy and detrimental to maximal output." [1] But it is obvious that not even the richest man can diminish in the slightest degree the noise of the streets of Paris or New York or Manchester, where even the fashionable quarters are often uncomfortably noisy. The noise of the great city can only be appreciably reduced by public

[1] C. S. Myers, *Mind and Work*, p. 67.

control, though hardly anything has as yet been done in this direction either in Europe or America.

Atmospheric pollution—" the smoke nuisance "—is another obvious example where one important condition of health is in any given place altogether beyond the purchase of private income, but definitely within the bounds of potential public control ; and here again the situation in England is unnecessarily backward, and far behind that of many other Western countries. A committee on Smoke and Noxious Vapours Abatement was recently appointed by the Ministry of Health, and made a valiant effort to express in terms of money income or " real " income the suffering and loss resulting from the prevalent methods of generating heat in the factory and home. In its Report the Committee pointed out that in Manchester, as compared with Harrogate, an extra cost of $7\frac{1}{2}$d. per week for fuel and washing was incurred by a working class home ; that the total loss for a city with a population of three-quarters of a million was £290,000 a year from this cause alone ; that much damage was done to metal work, textile fabrics and merchandise in general ; that much unnecessary repainting and redecorating was involved. At the end of this economic calculus the Committee, perhaps with a memory of the hideous dreariness of grime-laden streets and soot-covered interiors, perhaps aided by statistical calculations regarding the incidence of bronchial illnesses, suddenly abandoned the artificial method of evaluation which they had hitherto been using, and exclaimed that " it is clearly impossible to express in terms of money the damage to health and physical efficiency " arising from this evil.[1]

Even in the case of a simple article of everyday production and exchange, such as milk, the facts do not square with popular conceptions regarding the working of the economic machine. Although milk is of very great importance to the health of children and invalids, and to a lesser extent of adults, our belief in the efficacy of private income to control effectively the supply has up to the present prevented us from seriously tackling the question as a problem of public health, so that only a few half-hearted efforts in the way of collective action have so far found their way on to the Statute Book.[2] The result, in the words of the Astor Committee, is that " not only is the amount of milk consumed in Great Britain much lower than is desirable, but it is known that the quality as regards cleanliness has been, and is, gravely defective." [3] Over sixty per cent. of the milk which was recently

[1] Interim Report of the Committee on Smoke and Noxious Vapours Abatement, Cd 755, 1920, p. 3.

[2] The Milk and Dairies Act, 1915, which was a comprehensive measure, should strictly be excepted from this statement, for it did indeed find its way on to the Statute Book. But it was postponed and superseded ; and has never been put into operation.

[3] Final Report of the Committee appointed by the Board of Agriculture on the Production and Distribution of Milk. Cmd. 483/1919, p. 12.

being supplied even to the hospitals of Manchester was, as Professor Délépine discovered, scandalously impure.[1] In New York such milk could legally have been used only for cooking and manufacturing purposes, and its sale for consumption by children would have been prohibited. When we turn to the report of the Chief Medical Officer of Health we find that " the best conditions " for the production of milk were found, not in those places where average private income was highest, or where the largest number of wealthy individuals were gathered, but " in those districts in which the local sanitary authority showed most activity under the Dairy Orders." [2] In short, a proper supply of even a simple tangible commodity necessary to the preservation of health is not inevitably assured by the demand arising from the possessors of private income, and collective action and public expenditure may be required to satisfy that demand.

Although a great deal has already been achieved by the public medical service, much more could be done for itself by a nation which fully appreciated the vast potentialities of its own collective activities in this sphere. Nearly a decade ago Mr. Graham Wallas

[1] Final Report of the Committee appointed by the Board of Agriculture on the Production and Distribution of Milk. Cmd. 483/1919, p. 12 Details are also given of the excessive bacterial contents discovered in the milk supplied to twenty-one London hospitals.

[2] Annual Report of the Chief Medical Officer of the Ministry of Health, 1921, p. 79.

remarked that " if the State were willing to incur the necessary expense ringworm could be completely stamped out in England, and the present reason why it is not stamped out is that we have preferred to spend on Dreadnoughts the money which might have been given in subsidies for local medical treatment " [1] To-day, in post war England, the Chief Medical Officer of the Ministry of Health tells us that " the length of life of adult men in this country is much less than it should be, and there is no inherent reason why as much as three years should not be added to the average lifetime of Englishmen of 45." [2] The steps by which this addition to the span of life might be obtained nearly all involve an extension of public health activities in one direction or another, and an increased national expenditure upon them ; so that it may with some truth be said that if even the better-off classes of the community want to live longer they must be willing to yield up more of their income for collective health purposes than they do at present. Death is no respecter of income ; and even if it were true that the continuous enjoyment of considerable means resulted in a prolongation of life, this would hardly reassure the majority of business men. For the present economic order is defended largely on the debatable grounds that it enables men to rise from poor and obscure beginnings

[1] Graham Wallas, *The Great Society*, p. 176.
[2] Annual Report of the Chief Medical Officer, 1921, p. 21.

to positions of wealth and power and opportunity. The highly-placed in the economic ladder are, according to this view, chiefly drawn from the homes of the rank and file, and the length of their lives would therefore presumably be determined by the conditions governing the span of life of the humble folk from which they rose, comparatively late in life, rather than by the conditions governing the class into which they subsequently entered.

Quite apart from the question of the prolongation of life itself, and the elimination of diseases specially prevalent among children, such as ringworm, there is, to use the words of the Chief Medical Officer, " a wide prevalence of ill-health in the community due to general sickness, invalidity, and physical impairment . . . a great burden of disease . . . which finds no place in notification or death returns." [1]   In order to appreciate the nature and effect of these millstones of ill-health and poor physique, we must return once more to the medical survey made during the great war by the Ministry of National Service, to which reference has already been made in this chapter.   The medical examination for recruiting purposes of nearly two and a half million men resulted in the following allocation among the four grades of health : [2]

[1] Annual Report of the Chief Medical Officer of the Ministry of Health, 1921, p. 25.
[2] These grades have already been defined (see p. 30). The figure given of the number of medical examinations does not exactly

54

HEALTH

	Men.	Percentage.	Proportion.
In Grade I	871,769	36	1 in 3
In Grade II	546,276	22·3	1 in 5
In Grade III	756,859	31·2	1 in 3
In Grade IV	250,280	10·5	1 in 10
Total	2,425,184		

These figures denote that of every nine men of military age in Great Britain, on the average three are fit and healthy ; two exist upon a definitely inferior plane of health and strength ; three " could almost, in view of their age, be described as physical wrecks," ; and the remaining one is a chronic invalid with a precarious hold on life. Professor Keith devised a standard of physique of a very moderate character, which was for various practical purposes used and accepted by the expert members of the committee as a norm to which a reasonably healthy industrial nation such as Britain might be expected to approximate. Judged by Keith's standard, the Report states that our physical census showed " a shortage of 825,000

represent the number of men examined, for it included a certain number of re-examinations of the same men. Nevertheless, these repetitions were offset by certain other influences acting in a contrary direction. The original Report sets out fully the reasons why the statistics may be accepted as a substantially accurate estimate of the physical condition of a characteristic cross-section of the nation in normal times. See Ministry of National Service Report upon Physical Examination of men of military age, etc., Cmd. 504/1920, vol. i. p. 4.

Grade I men, an excess of 61,000 Grade II men, and the alarming excess of no less than 575,000 Grade III men, and 190,000 Grade IV men." [1]

These statements, made in an official report and based upon the hard logic of statistical method, are scarcely reassuring, or a fit subject for self-gratulation. They indicate in general, as the Report goes on to say, " the nature and extent of the ravages upon the health and physique of our manhood, which the progress of civilization during the nineteenth century has brought in its train." [2] Part of this physical ill-fare has been caused by the sacrifice of health to the process of income-getting; and this is what Professor Pigou appears to have in mind when he says that " perhaps the crowning illustration of this order of excess of trade over social net product is afforded by the work done by women in factories, particularly during the periods immediately preceding and succeeding confinement; for there can be no doubt that this work often carries with it, besides the earnings of the women themselves, grave injury to the health of their children." [3] A peculiar quality of tragedy is given to this kind of industrial activity by the fact that although the priceless element of health, both in the mother and the child, is easily sacrificed to the earning of an income, it cannot usually be repurchased at any price

[1] Ib. (see note 2, p. 54), p. 12. [2] Ib., p. 6.
[3] A. C. Pigou, *Economics of Welfare*, p. 163.

whatever. Nature holds the stakes, and knoweth not the money economy of men in their world.

We have already built up the essential foundations of a great public organization for the maintenance and creation of health in men and women and children. Behind the political machinery of democratic government stands a vast army of highly trained workers, often unrecognized and usually unknown, fighting a ceaseless battle with the forces which make for death and disease and decay. Appointed by, and responsible to, the popularly-elected district and county and borough councils are the regiments of medical officers and sanitary inspectors and district nurses ; the midwives, the school doctors, the analysts, the bacteriologists, the inspectors of nuisances, the asylum specialists, the tuberculosis experts, the dental surgeons, the sewage officials, the collectors of dust and garbage, the street cleaners. For the use of all these thousands of diverse public servants there exist, built and equipped and maintained at the orders of the elected representatives of the nation, hundreds of hospitals and clinics, asylums and sewage farms, maternity and child welfare centres, offices and storehouses. In the background looms the Ministry of Health, with its large staff of administrators and scientific experts, collating, advising and assisting the local departments of public health ; and behind that again stands the Medical Research Council of the Privy Council charged with the still greater function of tracing cause and effect, of revealing new truths in the dark cavern of the unknown.

The successes which might attend the efforts of this army, strengthened and enlarged, not only in the prevention of much of the " great burden of disease " which now hangs upon us, but also in the positive task of helping to create a more healthy, beautiful and vital nation in the future, are almost inconceivably great. But whatever further achievements are effected in this field will depend to a large extent upon our social outlook on the subject. It may therefore be desirable at this point to summarize the argument which has been pursued in this chapter.

Good health is an essential element of human welfare, but over and above a certain low point it does not necessarily or even normally increase perceptibly with increases of private income. The hygienic environment is to a large extent a common one for rich and poor alike, and hence most of the conditions of personal health depend more upon collective control and public expenditure than upon individual income. The public health service is essentially an " earning " service ; but the earnings are distributed in kind, and so do not enter into the monetary income of those who benefit. Very large measurable results have been achieved by collective action in regard to health, and it is definitely known that much more could be accomplished by an increase of conscious effort. But a

HEALTH

necessary condition of increased effort in this field is a realization that a diminution of private income may be more than compensated for by the receipt of a larger income in terms of health. Health cannot be calculated in terms of money or of so-called real income; and private income cannot purchase many of the essentials of physical well-being, although improved health may result in increased production and a larger earning power.

CHAPTER THREE

ART

LET us take next the æsthetic element, and consider its relation to private income in terms either of money or of the goods and services which constitute the " real " income of economists. In approaching this subject a certain fundamental agreement as to values must be taken for granted. No one can " prove," in any Euclidean sense of the word, that Bentham was wrong when he remarked that pushpin was as good as poetry; or demonstrate irrefutably that the Sistine Madonna of Raphael is superior to the coloured plates in *Pears' Annual;* or show beyond argument, in fact, that the entire province of art possesses any special worth at all. These things depend in the final analysis upon an inner perception which is beyond logic and above reason, upon an inherent sense of the relative values of certain things and the feelings which they evoke. It will be necessary, therefore, to assume during this discussion that the realm of æsthetic experience (in which I include not merely the fine arts, but all that pertains to the beautiful) is one which calls forth from the individual an emotional response of the purest and most refined quality, and that the

60

ability to partake of that experience is one of the most important elements in human welfare. Thus the cultivation of the artistic sense, by which I understand the ability both to appreciate and produce works of art, is an indispensable feature of any community which aspires to the good life. A serious difficulty in dealing with the subject arises from the fact that we have not so far discovered any method of quantitative measurement suited to the subject-matter; and for this reason it is usually neglected by social thinkers.

Although the appreciation of art (to take this aspect first) is a definite element in human well-being, its existence does not appear to depend upon private income to any very considerable extent, and the size of a man's income does not at all indicate whether or not he is accessible to the artistic appeal. The ability to perceive beauty is an innate quality which may be developed but which cannot be acquired. And although a larger income may bring, to a man or a woman who has only just enough for the necessities of life, increased opportunities for the development of æsthetic faculties in the form, for example, of greater leisure and freedom from preoccupation by petty cares, it is probable that most of the other activities made possible by increased private income do not actually result in an appreciable enlargement of the natural capacity of the owner for the recognition of artistic value.

The æsthetic pleasure which is derived from the

61

contemplation of a work of art has no relation either to the desire to acquire it or the pride of ownership which comes from actual possession. The essence of æsthetic experience is that disinterestedness which almost every writer on the subject, from Kant [1] onwards, has stressed. Sir Sidney Colvin, in an admirable article on the fine arts, remarks that " from the lowest point of the scale to the highest, we may observe that the element of personal advantage or monopoly in human gratifications seems to exclude them from the kingdom of fine art. The pleasures of fine art, so far as concerns their passive or receptive part, seem to define themselves as pleasures of gratified contemplation, but of such contemplation only when it is disinterested." [2] In another passage, speaking of these same pleasures again, he says that " they are not such as one human can in any sense receive exclusively from the object which bestows them. Thus it is evidently characteristic of a beautiful building that its beauty cannot be monopolized. . . . The same thing is true of a picture or a statue, except in so far as an individual possessor may choose to keep such a possession to himself, in which case his pride in exclusive ownership is a sentiment wholly independent of his pleasure in artistic contemplation." [3] Vernon

[1] Kant, *Critique of Æsthetic Judgment*, J. C. Meredith's Ed., Oxford Press, 1911, pp. 43–49.
[2] *Encyclopædia Britannica*, 11th Ed., vol. x. p. 357.
[3] Loc. cit.

ART

Lee, one of the most sensitive and acute writers on
art of our time, emphasizes the same fact when she
says that, as we reach maturity, " we learn that our
assimilation of beauty, and that momentary renewal
of our soul which it effects, rarely arises from our own
ownership; but comes, taking us by surprise, in
presence of hills, streams, memories of pictures, poets'
words, and strains of music, which are not, and cannot
be, our property. . . . Hence material possession has
no æsthetic meaning. We possess a beautiful object
with our soul; the possession thereof with our hand
or our legal rights brings us no nearer the beauty.
Ownership in this sense, may empower us to destroy
or to hide the object and thus cheat others of the
possession of its beauty, but does not help *us* to possess
that beauty." [1] Professor James Sully, writing in
the *Encyclopædia Britannica*, speaks of æsthetic experiences as " disinterested and universal modes of
enjoyment detached from personal interests . . .
clearly free from the egoistic exclusiveness which
characterizes our private enjoyments." [2]

Common experience appears to support this analysis
made by writers of authority. We do not feel that the
sense of rapture, the consciousness of something stirring
deeply within him, which the young clerk may feel when
he snatches half an hour from his lunch time in order

[1] *Laurus Nobilis*, by Vernon Lee, pp. 53–4.
[2] Article on Æsthetics in *Encyclopædia Britannica*, 11th Ed.,
vol. i. p. 280.

to look at his favourite Rembrandt in the city gallery is in any way diminished by the fact that it does not " belong " to him. And it is equally difficult to believe that the almost automatic acquisition of works of art by wealthy persons adds anything to their ability to perceive the beauty of those objects. Sir Montague Barlow, lately a Conservative cabinet minister, was reported as saying in a recent public address at the Victoria and Albert Museum that :[1] " He had a certain amount of experience of those who had made great fortunes in America. He would say for those who had amassed large fortunes in this country and in America that in his experience they were anxious to know. The fact that they did not know had often rather a pathetic side ; but they were anxious to secure the best and make great collections. He thought that was just as true in this country as in America." But the desire to " secure the best " and make a great collection has nothing to do with artistic appreciation. And in the same way the æsthetic emotion experienced by a millionaire when listening to a great musician is unaffected by whether the performance takes place at a public concert or, at great cost to himself, within the walls of his own home.

This absence of connexion between æsthetic exper-ience on the one hand and either the desire for owner-ship or the fact of possession on the other, is of great

[1] *The Times*, 21st July, 1923.

social importance. It enables us to realize that all the opportunities for artistic appreciation which are provided for the enjoyment of the community as a whole, irrespective of ability to pay, lend themselves to as acute a form of æsthetic experience as those which arise from private ownership. Hence it justifies such collective activities in the realm of art as national and municipal picture galleries, public concerts, beautiful buildings, bridges, monuments, statues, parks and gardens—always providing they are artistically successful. It also justifies the activities of those public-spirited men and women who fulfil a public function in a private capacity by donating to the nation works of art of various kinds.

Since ownership plays no part in the perception of artistic beauty, the size of a man's income is not likely to add considerably to his ability to partake of æsthetic experience. For the chief use made of private income is to exercise the power of acquisition. The old masters with which the wealthy man decorates his walls, the antique furniture, the Oriental rugs, the rare tapestries, the Chinese porcelain, the Indian carvings and all the other *objets d'art* which he is able to accumulate, may stimulate his love of display, and gratify his acquisitive instinct; but æsthetically they could be equally well enjoyed by him, if he is capable of appreciating them at all, in a museum or in an art gallery.

The real benefit which increases of income bring to

a person lies in the possibility of adapting his existence in such a way as to render his mind more sensitive to the emotional and intellectual processes which distinguish the creative artist. But this demands time and effort and a continuity of attention and interest, which is so rare in this connexion that very few men and women who possess relatively large incomes actually realize the potential opportunities for developing their æsthetic faculties which private wealth confers. The obstacles which interfere with this development in the lives of both rich and poor are suggested by Vernon Lee when she remarks that " in our still very badly organized world, an enormous number of people are condemned by the tyranny of poverty or the tyranny of fashion, to be, when the day's work or the day's business is done, in . . . a condition of fatigue and languor, of craving, therefore, for the baser kinds of pleasure. We all recognize that this is the case with what we call *poor people*, and that this is why poor people are apt to prefer the public house to the picture gallery or the concert room. It would be greatly to the purpose were we to acknowledge that it is largely the case with the rich, and that for that reason the rich are apt to take more pleasure in ostentatious display of their properties than in contemplation of such beauty as is accessible to all men." [1]

[1] *Laurus Nobilis*, by Vernon Lee, p. 24.

ART

The selfish monopoly, by private ownership, of opportunities for the perception of artistic beauty may actually detract from the pleasure which the owner himself can derive from them. " The culture of beauty and art," writes Professor James Sully, " has a socializing influence, helping to give to our emotional experience new forms of expression whereby our sympathies are deepened and enlarged." [1] And in another passage he remarks that " no one doubts that a man often enjoys beauty, e.g. that of a landscape, when alone ; yet at such a moment he not only recognizes that his pleasure is a possible one for others, but is probably aware of a subconscious wish that others were present to share his enjoyment. . . . As a rule we tend to indulge our æsthetic tastes in company with others." [2] The fact that the enjoyment of a beautiful thing is heightened by sharing is one which we know

[1] Article on Æsthetics in *Encyclopædia Britannica*, 11th Ed., vol. i. p. 285.
[2] Op. cit., p. 80. The passage continues : " This habit of making æsthetic enjoyment a social experience would in itself tend to develop the sympathies and the sympathetic intelligence and thus promote exchange of æsthetic experience. The content of our æsthetic experience would be favourable to such conjoint acts of æsthetic contemplation, and to the mutual sharing of æsthetic experiences, for, as disinterested and universal modes of enjoyment detached from personal interests, they are clearly free from the egoistic exclusiveness which characterizes our private enjoyments which at best can only be participated in by one or two closely attached friends. Our æsthetic enjoyments are thus eminently fitted to be social ones ; and as such they become greatly amplified by sympathetic resonance."

67

instinctively, says Vernon Lee, when, as children,
" we drag our comrades and elders to the window when
a regiment passes or a circus parades ; we learn it
more and more as we advance in life, and find we must
get other people to see the pictures, to hear the music,
to read the books which we admire." [1] It may not
be pure philanthropy which in England leads many
of the owners of great country houses to throw open
to the public at regular periods those rooms which
contain the art treasures ; or which in the United
States leads some of the wealthiest citizens to permit
their houses to be used as scenery for moving pictures
of a fictitious character.

If this conception of the essentially social nature of
æsthetic experience is well-founded [2] it would indicate
that an atmosphere favourable to both the appreciation
and the production of works of art can be and is in
fact largely brought about by the action of the
community as a whole.

The most striking point to be observed in connexion
with this aspect of the subject is that, particularly in
modern city life, the æsthetic environment is, like the
hygienic environment, to a large extent common to
both rich and poor—and this despite large differences
in artistic qualities between various districts within a

[1] *Laurus Nobilis*, by Vernon Lee, p. 50.
[2] See *L'Art au point de vue Sociologique*, par M. Guyau, Paris,
1889, for an elaborate analysis of this view, especially pp. 18–27.
Also Hennequin (quoted in Guyau, op. cit., p. 39).

single city. For this reason the social nature of æsthetic emotion is echoed, as it were, by an unavoidable sharing of feature and form by all who have eyes to see.[1] The most obvious illustration of this is to be found in civic architecture or town planning. Every inhabitant of London, rich or poor, if endowed with any sense of colour or form at all, has for years suffered acute discomfort from the artistic crime perpetrated by the designer and the constructors of the railway bridge at Charing Cross, whenever business or pleasure has brought him into its vicinity. Every citizen of Milan who is possessed of the most rudimentary artistic perception has all his life found pleasure, regardless of his income, in contemplating the marvellous cathedral which dominates that city.

The experience of the past century has shown that, in the existing economic order, our industrial towns and cities, when left to the unregulated self-interest of the capitalist *entrepreneur*, tend to develop into a hideous collection of slums and factories and office buildings which offend the eye and petrify the æsthetic faculties. The possessors of even the largest private incomes have been helpless in the face of so much deadweight of ugliness : they have been compelled either to endure it or to run away. It has been seen, frequently too late to prevent the mischief, that the

[1] An obvious example of this lies in the great mass of advertisements, most of them vulgar and ugly, which are displayed both in our city streets and country roads.

only remedy lies in social control; and actually it has been the community in its collective capacity which has been responsible for almost every town improvement scheme, every demolition of slum quarters, every attempt to widen and beautify the city streets, every effort to open up parks and recreation grounds, and in general for all measures intended to create a more artistic municipal environment. But neither the artistic disutilities involved in the ugliness produced by profit-seeking enterprise, nor the æsthetic satisfaction arising from the amenities brought into existence by collective action and public expenditure, find any expression in the money or real income of the individual.

It is not suggested that all public works and buildings are constructed with a conscious attempt at beauty; nor that all such attempts, where they are made, achieve success. Nevertheless, the tendency in collective action is for a stress to be laid upon artistic excellence, and we can see this illustrated in the case of corporate bodies such as the Universities of Oxford and Cambridge, or the Inns of Court.

The effect on the individual of the collective control of the common æsthetic environment may be considerable. One of the worst evils arising from the almost unrelieved ugliness of some of the industrial cities in the North of England is the atrophy of the æsthetic faculties of the inhabitants. Long habituation destroys all consciousness of the hideous nature of their surroundings ; and in Newcastle-on-Tyne, for example, I was unable during six months' residence to discover a single person aware of its artistic shortcomings. In a city such as Munich or Venice, on the other hand, where the municipality has concerned itself with creating and preserving a beautiful physical environment, there is a greater likelihood of a natural feeling for art in the individual being developed to a high point than in other circumstances. The enlightened American railroad magnate who wants his daughter to appreciate art does not keep her tied up in his house on Riverside Drive surrounded by costly treasures from all the auction rooms in Europe, but sends her to mix with the crowd in Dresden or Florence, where the atmosphere of prestige in which the fine arts are held, as symbolized by all the paraphernalia of civic beauty, will do more than anything else to quicken and develop any inherent æsthetic qualities which she may possess.

It is not owing to mere chance that, with a few trifling exceptions, all the finest churches, picture galleries, exhibitions of sculpture, museums, monuments, statues and buildings are public ones, provided for the most part by the community itself ; and that (at any rate up to the outbreak of the Great War) no opera company run for profit could compete artistically with the Hofoper in Vienna, nor any privately-owned theatre with the state theatre in Munich. The leading

English dramatists, actors and producers have for long believed that a public effort was required if a theatre was to be provided in England where the finest stage work could be performed.[1] In the National Gallery or the Louvre," writes Mr. Philip Wicksteed, " the poorest citizen who has the rudiments of artistic taste and culture may secure opportunities of enjoyment and education which no private collection could secure to even a handful of the community."[2] But the greater excellence and larger scale of the opportunities for æsthetic experience provided by the community in its collective aspect, as compared with those available to the resources of individual income, is not the only reason, or even the main reason, why the ability to appreciate works of beauty is more successfully fostered by social action than by private enterprise. Professor Patrick Geddes, generally regarded as our greatest authority on town planning, is acutely aware of the importance of the " atmosphere " when he says that " It is a mental illumination too, for our ' practical man ' to see (in Germany) natural beauty preserved, developed, rendered accessible to all, from river-front to mountain forest ; to see, too, that art is not something outside everyday life, something ' impractical ' at best to be grudgingly supplied in schools as a reputed aid towards the design of marketable commodities ;

[1] See *A National Theatre*, by H. Granville Barker and William Archer. Also *The Exemplary Theatre*, by H. Granville Barker.
[2] *The Commonsense of Political Economy*, by P. Wicksteed, p. 659.

but something to be viewed and treated as a worthy and social end in itself—in architecture, sculpture, and painting, in concert, drama and opera. To us, who so largely belong to towns greater in number of population and proportionately even richer than are these German ones, it is the most useful of experiences to see civic greatness estimated in more spiritual elements and public wealth more applied than with ourselves towards creating an environment of material beauty." [1]

It may be true, as an American writer suggests, that by emphasizing the æsthetic factor in our national culture and aims, much of the ugliness in our life "might be literally *voted* out of existence." [2] But to vote ugliness out of existence is not the same thing as to possess the power of creating positive beauty; and it is this latter aspect of æsthetic experience which we shall now consider.

The ability to produce works of art, accompanied by the desire to do so is, like the capacity to appreciate such works, a natural quality. It is of far greater rarity than the latter; but resembles it in that it may be developed but cannot be acquired. It is obvious that not the largest income in the world can enable a man to paint a fine picture or compose a great sonata unless he possesses certain inherent talents. And

[1] *Cities in Evolution*, by P. Geddes, pp. 214–15.
[2] *Art in Education and Life*, by H. Davies, published by Adams, Columbus, Ohio, 1914.

though the absence of financial means may sometimes prevent a born artist from training and developing his creative instincts to their highest point, the relation between individual income and artistic production is still more slender than the relation between income and æsthetic appreciation.

Ruskin, speaking of the fostering of the artistic genius, says " You dig him out as he lies nugget-fashion in the mountain stream ; you bring him home ; and you make him into current coin or household plate, but not one grain of him can you originally produce." [1]

In the world in which we live, however, the important question is not to what extent private income is able to endow its possessor with the talents of a creative artist, but rather to discover how far the desire for monetary gain, which is the incentive upon which the existing economic order is based, can be relied upon to persuade those who possess artistic genius to produce works of art. The ground of our enquiry is thus shifted from an examination of the relation between actual income and artistic talent to an investigation of the relation between the desire for or the expectation of monetary gain on the part of the artist and the work which he produces.

Although a young artist may be trained and given certain opportunities for doing creative work under comfortable conditions by a wealthy patron, the desire

[1] *The Political Economy of Art*, by John Ruskin, 1857 Ed., p. 30.

for private wealth, whether received as a gift in this way, or earned through the usual channels of commercial or professional exchange, does not usually provide an effective stimulus for the production of works of high art. Professor Taussig, though an economist, finds himself compelled to admit that " It is at least a question whether copyright has aroused genius or evoked literature " ;[1] and when Ruskin spoke of " that love of art which is the only effective patronage,"[2] he implied, as the aristocratic patrons of the fifteenth and sixteenth and seventeenth centuries well knew, that no hope of enrichment or favour will suffice to provide the incentive for the highest efforts unless the artist knows that the work he produces will be available for appreciation by a wide circle of the community.

The stimulus for the making of works of art is derived, primarily and essentially, not from the desire for private income, but from the public appreciation of art.[3]

[1] *Inventors and Moneygetters*, by F. W. Taussig, p. 18.
[2] *Modern Painters*, by J. Ruskin, vol. ii. p. 3, 1846 Ed.
[3] " The original or rudimentary type of lyric song and dancing arose when the first reveller clapped hands and stamped or shouted in time, in honour of his god, in commemoration of a victory, or in mere obedience to the blind stirring of a rhythmic impulse within him. To some very remote and ancestral savage the presence or absence of witnesses at such a display may in like manner have been indifferent ; but very early in the history of the race the primitive dancer and singer joined hands and voices with others of his tribe, while others again sat apart and looked on at the performance, and the rite thus became both choral and social. . . . The tendency of recent speculation and research concerning the origins of art has been to ascribe the primitive

THE RELATION OF WEALTH TO WELFARE

There may be other threads in the strand, but they are subordinate. We must distinguish, however, between the stimulating agent and the creative impulse of self-expression which is stimulated, though it is with the former that we are here concerned. "An artist composes mostly in order to obtain appreciation and applause ; this is his ruling passion," remarks Taine.[1] And Goethe, in the *Dichtung und Wahrheit*, says, " I do not deny, that if I thought of a happiness I would fain enjoy, the most fascinating shape in which it appeared to me was that of a laurel garland woven to adorn the poet's brow."[2] Ruskin, who devoted his whole life to the study of art, believed that " a great work is only done when the painter gets into the humour for it, likes his subject, and determines to paint it as well as he can, whether he is paid for it or not."[3] Henry Stephens, a friend and fellow student of Keats, tells us that Keats " had no idea of fame or greatness but as it was connected with the pursuits of poetry. . . . The greatest men in the world were

artistic activities of man less and less to individual and solitary impulse, and more and more to social impulse and the desire of sharing and communicating pleasure."—Sir Sidney Colvin, Article on " The Fine Arts," in *Encyclopædia Britannica*, p. 356, vol. x. 11th Ed. See also, on the need for an audience, *The Æsthetic Attitude*, by H. S. Langfeld, Harcourt, Brace, U.S.A., 1922, p. 266.

[1] *The Philosophy of Art*, by H. Taine, English Translation, New York, 1889, p. 102.

[2] *Poetry and Truth*, by J. W. von Goethe, English Translation by M. S. Smith, p. 142, vol. i. part i. book iv.

[3] *The Political Economy of Art* by J. Ruskin, p. 143.

the poets and to rank among them was the chief
object of his ambition." [1]   Beethoven was in some ways
a mercenary man ; but in a letter to his publishers he
wrote, " Rest assured that you are dealing with a true
artist who likes to be paid decently, it is true, but
who loves his own reputation and also the fame of his
art " ; [2] and in his diary he writes (after Pliny), " What
greater gift can man receive than fame, praise,
immortality." [3]

Dr. Johnson was a figure whose character, both as a
writer and as a man, was remarkably free from anything
approaching a susceptibility for the feelings which
other people might entertain towards him.   It is
therefore of particular interest to note the answer he
gave to the faithful Boswell on a certain occasion
when the latter refused to agree that a boy at school
was the happiest of human beings.   " I supported a
different opinion," writes Boswell, " from which I
have never yet varied, that a man is happier ; and I
enlarged upon the anxiety and sufferings which are
endured at school."   To which Johnson answered,
" Ah ! Sir, a boy's being flogged is not so severe as a
man's having the hiss of the world against him.   Men
have a solicitude about fame ; and the greater share
they have of it, the more afraid they are of losing it."

[1] Quoted in *The Life of John Keats*, by Sir Sidney Colvin, p. 31.
See also p. 139 for further evidence of Keats' desire for fame.
[2] *Beethoven, the Man and the Artist*, by F. Kerst, 1906, p. 79.
[3] Op. cit., p. 92.

THE RELATION OF WEALTH TO WELFARE

I silently asked myself (continued Boswell), " Is it possible that the great Samuel Johnson really entertains any such apprehension, and is not confident that his exalted fame is established upon a foundation never to be shaken ? " [1]

Shelley wrote nearly a whole poem on the feelings of an imaginative artist in relation to his work and the world, and declared in the second line of " An Exhortation " that

> Poets' food is love and fame.

Later in the same poem he writes :

> Fame is love disguised : if few
> Find either never think it strange
> That poets range.

> Yet dare not stain with wealth or power
> A poet's free and heavenly mind.

And Milton, in " Lycidas," says :

> Fame is the spur that the clear spirit doth raise
> (That last infirmity of noble mind)
> To scorn delights, and live laborious days.

Mr. Arnold Bennett is a contemporary author who is something of an epicure in describing methods of spending money, and he has frankly admitted that he desired to obtain considerable wealth from his own literary work. But he reveals the importance in his own case of social appreciation when he says that, at a

[1] Vol. i. p. 451.

certain period, " Many people took care to read almost all that I wrote. But my name had no significance for the general public. The mention of my name would have brought no recognizing smile to the average person who is 'fond of reading.' I wanted to do something large, arresting, decisive." [1]

This need for the social recognition of the art impulse may be seen even in children. " No invention pleases them," observes Professor Baldwin, " until it is socially confirmed by mother or sister. No attainment —drawing, new speech combination, hand manipulation, or what-not of youthful pride—is of much value, or held in high esteem, until father has seen that his boy can do it and do it by himself. His sense of agency or originality seems to feed and grow fat upon just the sort of recognition which comes through his exhibition of himself in his social circle. . . . The exhibition of his new drawing in the home circle is as much to his budding genius as is the exhibition which the artist makes in the Salon." [2]

Although neither the expectation, nor the actual acquisition, of monetary gain can provide the stimulus for the best creative art work, private wealth may sometimes enable a painter or an author or a poet to respond to that stimulus. But even that service appears to be rare. Yet this is not to say that the

[1] *The Truth about an Author*, by Arnold Bennett, p. 148.
[2] *Social and Ethical Interpretations in Mental Development*, by J. M. Baldwin, 1897, Macmillan, New York, p. 149.

desire for gain plays no part in directing the activities
of the creative artist. Artists, like other people, have
to live ; and are indeed at times even more unscrupulous and extravagant in money matters than the general
run of humanity. When money needs predominate
the artist will either " stoop to qualify creation by
much imitative repetition " [1] or confine his talents to
certain profitable fields, or frankly "potboil." Mr.
Joseph Thorp relates how he once asked Mr. Frank
Brangwyn, the distinguished painter and etcher, why
he did not design a carpet. "Because nobody will
pay me for it. At least no English firm," [2] was the
reply. A similar restriction of the field of activity
was indicated by Beethoven, when he wrote " I do
not write what I most desire to do, but that which I
need to because of money. But this is not saying
that I write only for money." [3] Perhaps a more
typical example of the attitude of a conscientious artist
toward his work and its remuneration is that revealed
by Samuel Butler, in a letter to his friend, Mr. F. G.
Fleay, on the subject of " Erewhon," which is generally
regarded as his greatest achievement. " As regards
the selling of the book," he wrote, " while writing it

[1] *Work and Wealth*, by J. A. Hobson, p. 46.
[2] From a letter on " Art in Industry " in *The Times*, 2nd July,
1923. Mr. Brangwyn went on to say, Mr. Thorp writes, that a
German firm had offered him a couple of hundred guineas for
designing a carpet, which he had accepted.
[3] *Beethoven, the Man and the Artist*, by F. Kerst, p. 46.

I never gave money a thought, but aimed solely at efficiency. *Now* I desire to gain as much by it as ever I can, and in price, etc., should be guided almost entirely by the consideration of how to make most money out of it for myself." [1]

The fact that financial considerations may induce an artist to confine his activities to certain kinds of work, or to produce work of an inferior quality because it "pays," indicates that the influence of money upon the artist is negative rather than positive ; and is not inconsistent with the statement that the fundamental stimulus for the production of the finest art work is the desire for a widespread social recognition. A distinction has already been drawn between the stimulating agent and the impulse which is stimulated.

" Originality in art," writes Professor Baldwin, " is an affair both of individual endowment and thought and of social recognition and confirmation . . . The reaction of this social recognition upon the producer is not alone the fountain of his stimulus and the test of his success ; it is also the very source of his sense of values." [2] The powerful influence exerted by the community over the creative artist either by yielding or withholding this social recognition may be traced with some exactitude in certain cases ; though to what

[1] Correspondence reproduced in *The Times*, 18th September, 1923.
[2] *Social and Ethical Interpretations in Mental Development*, by J. M. Baldwin, p. 150.

extent this is modified by the excellence or inferiority of the prevailing artistic standards is not known. Every theatre manager knows that when business is bad he must fill the house with non-paying "dead-heads" if the quality of the performance is to be maintained, although the actors' remuneration is usually fixed irrespective of the size of the audience; and Mr. St. John Ervine, the playwright and critic, has said that "The first necessity in the creation of great drama is a great audience."[1] The knowledge that a quarter of a million persons had bought copies of a cheap edition of his book would produce in almost every literary artist a much stronger stimulus to the further exploitation of his powers than the knowledge that a handful of wealthy persons had purchased a few hundred copies in an expensive edition *de luxe*, even if the monetary reward were the same in both cases. "My own pleasure in production was boundless," wrote Goethe, "but when in the society of appreciative friends, I recalled what I had written to myself and others, my delight in it was renewed. Moreover, many took an interest in my longer and shorter works, because I always urged anyone who felt in any degree inclined to write and fitted for it, to produce something independently, in his own vein, and was, in my turn, continually incited by everyone

[1] In a Syllabus of his Lecture on " The Drama and the Audience "; at King's Hall, London, 6th November, 1923.

to fresh compositions in prose and verse. This mutual spurring and egging on to effort, even carried to an extreme as it was, gave everyone a happy influence of his own ; and from this whirl of creative energy . . . this give and take . . . arose that extolled and decried, yet far-famed epoch in literature." [1] Albrecht Dürer, a supremely great artist of the Renaissance, writing from Venice in 1506 to Master Wilibald Pürkheimer, a Burgher of his own native city of Nuremberg, cries, with an unusual outburst of passion, " Oh, how I shall freeze after this sun ! Here I am a gentleman, at home a parasite." [2] What Dürer meant was that in Venice there was a more widespread recognition of the value of art than existed in the Germany of his day ; and the consciousness of being regarded as one whose work was felt to be significant by the general public was of definite importance in his life.

Taine, analysing the social phenomena which resulted in the greatest period of the Italian Renaissance, describes how Italy then had, almost contemporaneously, not only a handful of artists of unique genius, such as Leonardo Da Vinci, Michael Angelo, Raphael, Gorgione, Titian, Veronese, Correggio, but also a " brotherhood of eminent and accomplished painters . . . and a hundred others less known . . . and

[1] *Dictung und Wahrheit* (*Poetry and Truth*, English Translation by M. S. Smith), vol. ii. p. 66.
[2] Letters from Venice in *Records of Journeys to Venice and the Low Countries*, by A. Dürer. Edited by Roger Fry, Boston, 1912.

finally, around these families of artists, so diversified and so faithful, a crowd of connoisseurs, patrons and buyers, a vast public forming an escort, not alone of gentlemen and cultivated people, but of townsmen, artisans, simple monks, and the commonalty ; so that fine taste, at this epoch, was natural, spontaneous, universal, the entire community, in its sympathy and intelligence, contributing to the works which the masters signed with their names." [1]   Sir Sidney Colvin, in his biographical record of the influences which led Keats to forsake medicine for poetry, says that " Keats found among those with whom he lived nothing to check, but rather everything to foster, his hourly growing, still diffident and half awe-stricken, passion for the poetic life.   Poetry, and the love of poetry were at this period in the air.   It was a time when even people of business and people of fashion read ; a time of literary excitement, expectancy, discussion and disputation, such as England has not known since." [2]

The extent to which an atmosphere, favourable or unfavourable to the production of art, can be brought about by the action and the attitude of the community as a whole, and the degree to which this atmosphere is independent of money income, may be illustrated by the example of certain modern countries.

Before the war of 1914–18 Great Britain was the

[1] *Lectures on Art*, by H. Taine, Translated New York (H. Hold), 1884, pp. 22–3.
[2] *Life of John Keats*, by Sir Sidney Colvin, p. 83.

wealthiest country in the world; but it would be difficult to imagine witnessing anywhere in England the scene I saw in Verona, when over eighty thousand peasants and manual workers paid hard-earned money in order to listen, in breathless appreciation, to a superb performance of the opera " Aïda " given in the open-air arena erected by the ancient Romans in that city.

Average income in the United States of America is higher than in any other country in the world; but the American nation lives artistically for the most part on European culture. " The most moving and pathetic fact in the social life of America to-day is emotional and æsthetic starvation," [1] is what we read in the introduction to a symposium which attempts a conscious evaluation of civilization in the States. " America has produced no work of imagination of the first order," writes Mr. Davies, a former lecturer in æsthetics in Yale University, " not a single work of art ranking in the first class, a work, that is, at once original, unique, and stamped with a distinctly American spirit, has ever been produced in this country." [2] Speaking of music, Mr. Deems Taylor remarks that America spends more money upon music than does any other nation on earth, and that some of the orchestral and operatic per-

[1] *Civilization in the United States*, An Enquiry by Thirty Americans, Harcourt, Brace & Co., p. 7.

[2] *Art in Education and Life*, by H. Davies, p. 5, published by Adams, Columbus, Ohio.

formances are unsurpassed ; but, he adds, " there has never been a successful opera by an American offered at that opera house, and the number of viable American orchestral works is small enough to be counted almost upon one's fingers. We squander millions upon an art that we cannot produce." [1] Later he explains that " the total unconsciousness on the part of his fellow countrymen that art is related to life, a sense of futility and unreality, is what makes the lot of the musician in America a hard one, and is responsible for his failure as an artist." [2] Mr. George Jean Nathan, a New York dramatic critic, observes that " In no civilized country in the world to-day is there among playwrights so little fervour for sound drama as in the United States. . . . The American professional theatre is to-day at once the richest theatre in the world, and the poorest." [3] Speaking of literature in America, Mr. Van Wyck Brooks tells a similar tale : " The aspect of our contemporary literature . . . is indeed one long list of spiritual casualties. It is not that the talent is wanting, but that somehow this talent fails to fulfil itself." [4] The reason for this he believes is that the American writer is " insufficiently equipped, stimulated, nourished by the society into which he has been born." [5] Mr. Walter Pach, himself a well-known etcher and painter, tries to explain why

[1] *Civilization in the United States*, article on " Music," p 199.
[2] Op. cit., p. 207.
[3] Op. cit., p. 249.
[4] Op. cit., p. 181.
[5] Op. cit.,p. 183.

the social environment of American life is so antithetic to artistic creation. He refers to the various forms of " collective action of an artistic character " which are to be found in Europe, and argues that in the old world " the exceptional individual, born with a strong instinct towards art, has surroundings and a foundation that are lacking here." He observes later that " we cannot expect an art really representative of America until there is a foundation of regard for his works that the artist can build on." [1] This condemnation of the æsthetic environment in the United States by American writers is more severe than any criticism which a visitor from abroad would venture to make ; but, whether it is a just estimate or an exaggeration, it certainly affords an explanation of the remarkable disparity between the great economic prosperity of the United States on the one hand and the feeble output of creative art which emerges from that country on the other.

Professor Patrick Geddes laments that once " Scottish singers and thinkers also were known throughout their land and beyond : but that was in times of comparative poverty." [2] Yet it would be wrong to assume that industrial and commercial prosperity is necessarily inimicable to the development of the fine arts. The period of great artistic production in ancient

[1] Op. cit., pp. 229–30.
[2] *Cities in Evolution*, by P. Geddes, p. 81.

Greece was also a period of material wealth relative to the standards then existing. The Renaissance in Italy coincided with a time of notable economic activity in Venice, Florence and the other great Italian art centres. The classic school of Dutch painting flourished mainly in the early seventeenth century, when Holland was one of the greatest, if not actually the greatest, trading country in Europe. In England the glorious outburst of the æsthetic impulse which expressed itself in Tudor architecture and Elizabethan literature occurred at a time which also witnessed a considerable expansion of overseas trading ventures. So that it is clear that, although creative talent in the realm of art cannot be purchased in the ordinary sense of the word, the possession of surplus wealth over and above the necessities of life may be fruitfully employed in enabling artists to respond to the stimulus which is derived from the hope or from the fact of social appreciation of their work. What appears absolutely certain is that at no time has a great body of art work of high quality been produced in the absence of a widespread contemporary appreciation.

The relation between the attitude of the community towards art in general (with particular reference to the consideration of the common æsthetic environment) and the development of the essential qualities of good citizenship, is well brought out by Mr. Graham Wallas, when he reminds us that if " children still in school

are to be taught what Mr. Wells calls the ' sense of the
State ' we may, by remembering Athens, get some
indication of the conditions on which success depends.
Children will not learn to love London while getting
figures by heart as to the millions of her inhabitants
and the miles of her sewers. If their love is to be
roused by words, the words must be as beautiful and
as simple as the chorus in praise of Athens in the
Œdipus Ooloneus. But such words are not written
except by great poets who actually feel what they
write, and perhaps before we have a poet who loves
London as Sophocles loved Athens it may be necessary
to make London itself more lovely." [1] Yet London
can only be made more lovely by the efforts of artists
who, like Sophocles, express what they feel, though in
another medium ; and thus the task is but removed
one stage farther back. No group of artists is likely
to have the " feeling " and the continuity of creative
impulse that will result in a more beautiful city unless
they are at once the inspiration and the echo of the
inarticulate yearnings of the mass of plain men and
women who crowd the common streetways in the
gathering dusk, stirred perhaps, for all their weariness,
by the sudden glory of the setting sun as it throws its
crimson mantle over the outline of a building inherited
from an age which may have known better than our own
wherein lie the deepest satisfactions of the human soul.

[1] *Human Nature in Politics,* by G. Wallas, p. 193.

THE RELATION OF WEALTH TO WELFARE

The argument which has been pursued in this chapter attempts to show that although the æsthetic factor is an element of supreme value in human welfare it is not directly related to individual income. The ability to appreciate artistic beauty is an inherent individual quality which is as a rule more effectively developed by a solicitude on the part of the community as a whole for the common æsthetic environment than by increases in private income. Æsthetic contemplation has a social quality which may even prevent a person who selfishly monopolizes opportunities for artistic enjoyment from deriving the fullest possible satisfaction from them. The benefits which result from social action in the realm of art, and the ill-fare which comes from a disregard for æsthetic considerations, find no place in private income. The ability to create works of art is also an inherent natural faculty unconnected with private wealth. It cannot be evoked by either the expectation, or the actual possession, of private fortune. Individual income may sometimes enable an artist to respond to the stimulus to creative effort, but the stimulus itself is provided chiefly by the desire for public appreciation. The social recognition of the artist and his work is an influence of the utmost importance as an aid to the development of natural artistic genius, and the attitude of the community can bring about an atmosphere favourable or unfavourable to the production of art. This " attitude " may or may not be accompanied by material prosperity, but it is distinct from a mere readiness on the part of wealthy persons to spend sums of money on the acquisition of works of art. The welfare derived from a phase of great artistic productiveness, and the deprivation which exists in a period of æsthetic stagnation, find no place in the money or real income of individuals.

VARIATIONS ON THE THEME

CHAPTER FOUR

WORK

IN most western countries about a third of the entire lifetime of nearly all men, and of a very large number of women, is occupied by work ; and we shall now consider work as an element of welfare, and from that aspect examine its relation to income. The word " work " is used as a generic term for an immense diversity of human activities, many of which have almost nothing in common with one another. One man's work will be another man's play. A professional cricketer will regard the daily practice and the weekly match as his work ; and if two men are climbing a mountain in Switzerland the expedition will be recreation to the tourist but work to the guide. Work cannot be defined as comprising those activities which are actually gainful to the individual, or from which he hopes to achieve financial gain ; for an unpaid County Councillor may accurately describe six hours spent in committee and council chamber as " a hard day's work," though it brings him no personal reward in this sense. Married women, on the other hand, are frequently irritated because their husbands refuse to regard housekeeping as " work," chiefly because it yields a return which is not paid for in the ordinary way by the consumer, but is enjoyed in kind by the producer and her family. Apart, however, from women's work in the home (and even here an exception must be made in the case of domestic servants and nurses for children) most of the great mass of activities which we call work are those for which earnings are received, in the form either of wages, salaries, fees or profits ; and it is with this kind of work that we shall be mainly concerned.

In spite of the fact that so large a portion of the average person's life is spent at work in office or field, shop or factory, mine or ship, wagon or warehouse, one of the outstanding features of modern life is the scant attention that is given to the relation between the work and the worker. The result is that the majority of people find their daily work a distasteful grind or a dull routine ; and most of them imagine that this is somehow inevitable.

The economists have been exceptionally narrow in their whole treatment of the subject. Marshall, writing in the last quarter of the nineteenth century, remarked that " The true reward which an occupation offers to labour has to be calculated by deducting the money value of all its disadvantages from that of all its advantages : and we may describe this true reward as the *net advantages* of the occupation." [1]

[1] A. Marshall, *Principles of Economics*, 8th Ed., p 73.

But neither the disadvantages which arise when a man who is by nature a musician is forced by the pressure of circumstances into a soap-boiling factory, and is made unhappy as a result; nor the advantages which accrue when he is able to follow his bent, can be calculated in terms of money. Professor Pigou, in a recent book, says " non-economic welfare is liable to be modified by the manner in which income is earned. For the surroundings of work react upon the quality of life. Ethical quality is affected by the occupations —menial service, agricultural labour, artistic creation, independent as against subordinate economic positions." [1] That is to say, Professor Pigou admits that the processes by which economic wealth is produced have a vital effect upon human well-being, but regards that effect as relating to " non-economic welfare," and as lying therefore outside the sphere of economic science.

The first aspect of work which we shall consider will be the relation between the capacity of the worker and the function which he fulfils. A close correspondence between inborn capacity and industrial function is a fundamental element in human welfare; but except in the case of exceptionally successful men and women in the professions, there is, in our insufficiently organized society, only a slender relationship between the extent of this correspondence and the amount of

[1] A. C. Pigou, *Economics of Welfare*, p. 14.

income. No one can tell from the size of his income whether a cloth merchant has a natural bent for commercial enterprise and finds his work interesting, or whether he was cajoled or coerced into business by a father who regarded the youthful leanings of his son towards natural history as a boyish whim of no consequence. But if he has a distaste for business, no increase of income will make the work itself more interesting to him, though he may succeed in accumulating a fortune therefrom. A research chemist, struggling to make two ends meet on an annual income rather less in amount than that earned by a bank director in a month, may derive, from the opportunity to pursue his craving for scientific investigation, a satisfaction which not the largest income could yield him if it necessitated a different employment of his working hours.

It is true that under existing economic conditions a person earns what he is " worth " in any given occupation ; because in the present state of society we regard a person's economic services as being " worth " just what they will fetch in the market ; so that a person earns what he is worth and is worth what he earns. In this sense there is a close approximation between earnings and efficiency, whether natural or acquired, in any given occupation. But the choice of an occupation and the attainment of a high position therein at present often depend more largely upon inherited opportunity than upon inherent capacity ; for as Mr. Graham Wallas remarks, " in any million of members in a modern industrial nation it is not likely that more than one of the twenty who are best fitted to be inventors, or writers, or organizers, or explorers, or artisans, receives the necessary training and opportunity." [1] In consequence, in contrast to the approximation between earnings and actual efficiency, there is a wide disparity between earned income and potential efficiency.

There is a fairly widespread recognition of the desirability of enabling an individual of obvious and clearly defined genius to utilize his natural talents, though no adequate effort is made by the community to bring about that result. But the vast majority of men and women are not possessed of a distinct and well-marked bent in any one direction, and in their case there is little appreciation of the need for that careful and expert investigation of inherent characteristics which is required if a correspondence between function and capacity is to be obtained. Yet such an investigation is necessary in the case of every worker, because " for each individual " as a distinguished psychologist has said, " there is one occupation which is more suitable than any other." [2] The less clearly defined the indications of specific ability, the greater the need for discovering them by scientific method.

[1] *Our Social Heritage*, by Graham Wallas, p. 93:
[2] *Mind and Work*, by C. S. Myers, pp. 85–6.

WORK

A certain amount of work has already been done by psychologists in this field ; and one of the results has been to establish the fact that the advantages arising from a correspondence between function and capacity, and the disadvantages arising from haphazard methods of selection, apply throughout the whole field of industry, from the original creative specialist down to the humblest routine worker. A special investigator of the Industrial Fatigue Research Board, in a report dealing with sweet factories, tells us that " Packers are generally chosen on account of their nice hands, and such workers as apply and have not ' nice hands ' are put on to other work such as is done in the packet and dipping departments." But, the writer goes on to suggest, " there are psychological factors at work which prevent a worker whose physical qualities are well adapted to the work from doing really well at it." [1] From a report on the printing trade we learn that individual differences in efficiency among hand compositors are " largely due, in the last resort, to the relative carelessness often shown in accepting apprentices, the result being that a number of boys become ' printers ' who are not suited for printing, and, after having drifted into the industry, they remain as inefficient hand compositors." [2] This lack of correspondence between capacity and function, disastrously wasteful

[1] Report No. 16 of the Industrial Fatigue Research Board, *Three Studies in Vocational Selection*, 1922, p. 85
[2] Ib., p. 6.

both to the individual and to the community, is brought about by the normal methods of economic selection at present prevailing. "A works manager," the report goes on to say, "however 'cautious' he may be, neglects to determine to what extent a boy is *naturally fitted* for a printer. This is at present inevitable, as we have not been provided with any means of doing so. His examination of a boy consists in testing roughly certain *acquisitions*, spelling, grammar, etc., and while these are important, natural endowments are more important. The present more or less rough methods of testing knowledge (and character) might . . . be supplemented by an exact method of determining aptitudes." [1]

An increasing amount of attention is being paid in the United States to the problem of discovering specific capacity, and of directing it into the appropriate occupation. The President of Chicago University, in a recent Annual Report, lays special stress on the importance of stimulating students of *average* ability in the direction of their natural aptitudes. "The largest class of students—those of average ability—also requires more attention," he remarks. "The special problem in this group is that of waking up the individual to his responsibility to his future self and to the opportunity in his present situation. This

[1] Op. cit., pp. 33–4. A series of suggested tests for determining aptitudes is given in the report.

98

requires personal and intimate conference. Recently
a student entered my office for the purpose of dropping
a Spanish course. As usual I began by asking what
he expected to do on leaving college. ' Oh, I don't
know. My people want me to be a physician, and I'm
taking a pre-medical course. But I don't want to
be a doctor.' ' Well, what interests you ? ' ' Zoology ;
but a fellow can't be just a zoologist.' ' Indeed ?
Did you ever think of being a curator of the department
of zoology in a museum ? ' He straightened himself
in his chair and listened excitedly while I told him of
a friend who was just such a curator. I gave him a
card of introduction to a curator in the Field Museum.
With considerable enthusiasm he started to go, and
turning said : ' What about this Spanish ? Hadn't
I better drop it now ? ' ' My friend spent last winter
collecting in South America.' Then, with a vigour of
diction . . . he said, ' I get you ! ' In other words,
two things had happened to this lad : his will became
engaged in preparation for future work, and he saw
the relationship to that work borne by a college
course."[1] What he also perceived, perhaps unconsciously, was that not all the thousands a year which a
large medical practice might bring him could yield

[1] Report of President of Chicago University, 1921–2, p. 27.
The passage concludes : " Such conference ought to be possible
with every student. The organization of such guidance on a
large scale involves the deans, possibly a personnel office including
responsibilities for vocational guidance, placement, and alumni
relations, and all members of the faculties.":

also the unique and irreplaceable satisfaction which comes to an individual whose working hours are passed in doing that for which he is best equipped by nature and training, whether it be hand compositing, or arranging zoological exhibits in a museum, or turning pistons on a lathe, or tending the flower beds in a public park, or writing poetry, or regulating the traffic in a crowded city, or driving a motor lorry, or delivering letters in a country district.[1] Some kinds of work appear intolerably monotonous to most people, but Henry Ford[2] has shown that, in the first place, it can be alternated with other work without loss of efficiency, under even the most highly specialized conditions ; and in the second place, that some workers prefer to remain at apparently monotonous tasks rather than to take advantage of an opportunity to make a change.

Mr. Graham Wallas points out that one of the necessary conditions of social contentment is " a greater positive liking by men and women for the work they do,"[3] and also that " an almost unimaginable increase of personal happiness, social contentment, and economic efficiency would result if the achievement of a more complete adjustment [between capacity and function] became the conscious organized and effective purpose of modern civilization."[4]   But such an adjustment

[1] See *Our Social Heritage*, by Graham Wallas, p. 93.
[2] *My Life and Work*, by H. Ford, p. 106.
[3] *Our Social Heritage*, by Graham Wallas, p. 90.   [4] Ib., p. 93.

will not become the conscious purpose of society unless
certain of the ideas current in western countries are
revised. The common conception of work as being a
mere means of earning an income in terms of money
must be widened so as to embrace the notion of the
" income " in satisfaction, or the loss in dissatisfaction
which the worker himself derives from his task.
" Vocational guidance," runs a report of the Industrial
Fatigue Research Board, " if it is to play a helpful
part in industry, must take a very long view, and it
should be realized that the work of those engaged in
it is not to get immediate results, but to see that the
whole life of a worker be used to the best advantage,
both for himself and the community, and not, as is
too often the case, that his young energy should be
sapped up in an occupation he is not really fitted for." [1]
Vocational guidance of this order is a form of social
organization which can only be carried out successfully
by the community in its collective capacity, acting
either through the central government, co-ordinated
local authorities, public educational bodies, or impartial
scientific and administrative commissions set up by
the State. It involves the abandonment, to a very
large extent, of the belief that the unregulated drive
and inducement, the haphazard pressure and suction,
of the competitive economic system provides a satisfactory method of selecting human material for

[1] Report No. 16, *Three Studies in Vocational Selection*, 1922, p. 86.

industrial purposes, of corelating natural capacity and productive function in a manner conducive to the maximum welfare either of society or of the individual. Furthermore, it involves a drastic change in the distribution of opportunity, and the source from which it arises. To-day the opportunity for a young man or girl to enter an occupation is to a very large degree determined by the wealth, education, and social position of the parents; and in this sense is chiefly an inherited advantage or disadvantage. At the poorer end of the scale the choice of possible careers is limited, or strongly influenced, save in the case of quite exceptional genius, by the poverty, immediate needs, short-sightedness or ignorance of the parents; and at the richer end of the scale by their avarice, snobbishness, social ambition or enslavement to fashion. The irreparable loss in welfare which is suffered by a child of the slums whose natural faculties are thwarted by unsuitable work is often recognized; but among the wealthier classes of society there are very many men who are also square pegs in round holes so far as their work is concerned, and who stand equally in need of sympathy on that account. Both rich and poor need not only a widened sphere of opportunity, but the occupational training and modified outlook which would also be required if full advantage were to be taken of a greater freedom of choice.

Vocational guidance aims at solving the problem all

along the line, for poor and wealthy alike ; but it can do so only on conditions that are relentlessly antithetic to our existing economic philosophy. It is obviously a waste of time to discover, by elaborate physical and psychological tests, the natural aptitude of boys and girls who are about to enter the working arena of modern life, unless it is intended to train and develop those faculties for their appropriate employemnt. Thus it follows that the embryonic composer must receive a long musical education without reference to the obscure poverty of his parents ; the girl with the longing and the ability to tend sick people must become a hospital nurse, no matter how elegant her home surroundings ; the duke's son with the makings in him of a factory inspector must lose ' caste ' in order to attain well-being.

We pass now to the consideration of an entirely different aspect of the subject. The welfare of a man in regard to his work is seriously affected by his status ; and in modern western civilization status is largely determined by occupation. The connexion between income and status is a slender one. It is impossible to ascertain a person's status from a mere knowledge of his or her income ; and in the economic or professional sphere increases of income are often unaccompanied by improved status, and vice versa. In the fighting services there exists, alongside a remarkable inequality in rank, pay, responsibility and authority, a fundamental equality of status ; and the status of a combatant officer of any rank is in England regarded as being higher than that of even the richest business man.

The question of economic status is one which has become increasingly prominent of late years in Europe, and the aim of most associations of producers, whether trade unions or professional organizations, is to secure an improvement in the standing of their members. The chief cause of this appears to be a consciousness on the part of large numbers of workers that the industrial revolution has resulted in their being regarded, not as human beings possessed of certain productive capacities, but as mere industrial categories endowed with subordinate human qualities. In the machine industry, says Professor Taussig, "The relation between employer and employee inevitably becomes impersonal and mechanical. The workman is no longer Bill Jones ; he becomes a number on the payroll. From it all there emerges, or at least is accentuated, an attitude towards work quite different from that of the independent craftsman or of the small-scale employer." [1] Mr. Frank Hodges, until recently secretary of the Miners' Federation of Great Britain, in a little book which may be regarded as expressing the feelings current among the million coal miners who

[1] *Inventors and Money-getters*, by F. W. Taussig, p. 65.

belong to the Federation, remarks " During the era of modern capitalism the miners have enjoyed the status enjoyed by other workers, precisely the same status as that enjoyed by inanimate raw material, or by horses and asses engaged in production. The working class has stood in the market place. Its own person was the commodity, labour power, that labour power was for sale, and a human personality went with the transaction." [1]

Whether this is a true or an exaggerated view of the position occupied hitherto by the industrial worker it is beside our purpose to discuss. What is undeniable is that great masses of manual and clerical workers believe it to be approximately a true presentation ; and men and women act on their beliefs rather than according to the logic of objective fact. It is certain that large bodies of organized workers feel that status is a definite element of welfare in their lives, and they regard it as a factor which is independent of increases or decreases of income. " Even when the wage earner is getting what he calls ' good money ' and steady work," write Mr. and Mrs. Webb, " he resents the fact that he, like the machine with which he works, is bought as an instrument of production." [2]

The demand for improved status appears to arise fundamentally from a desire on the part of the worker

[1] *Nationalization of the Coal Mines*, by F. Hodges, p. 111.
[2] *The Decay of Capitalist Civilization*, by Sidney and Beatrice Webb, p. 48.

to be recognized primarily as a human being rather than as a " hand." In England, says Mr. J. A. Hobson, this demand might mean " anything from recognition of the Union to an equal voice with the employer in the management. . . . Its minimum actual significance, however, is a demand that labour shall have a ' real ' or perhaps an equal voice with ' capital ' in determining the conditions of employment of labour." [1]

In the United States of America, where a demand of this kind would be much less widely supported, more strongly resisted, and far less likely to succeed than in Great Britain, many employers who are invincibly opposed even to the recognition of Labour Unions, are endeavouring to invest their employees with a sense of personality in their work. The dining cars on most of the railways contain a framed notice announcing the name of the steward in charge in language which is courteous to the steward as well as to the public. In New York City I observed a motor omnibus conductor wearing a gilt and enamel badge inscribed " Mr. Irving Brink," and underneath were the words " service, loyalty, civility." Mr. Brink was the conductor, and it was the custom of the motorbus

[1] *Incentives in the New Industrial Order*, by J. A. Hobson, p. 106. " This demand," Mr. Hobson says, " means something more than wage and hours' contracts. It includes questions of the use of machinery, dilution, workshop discipline and provisions against unemployment, and involves the establishment of some regular and representative body in the workshop operating this ' status.' "

corporation to give each one of their conductors a specially made badge of this kind. An advertisement inserted recently by one of the great transatlantic shipping lines in a New York newspaper,[1] contained a pen and ink portrait of Mr. F. V. Jones, the chief steward of one of the company's liners, and spoke of him as " omnipresent, tireless, and unfailingly cheerful." The " personal sense of satisfaction " which the company assured prospective passengers they would enjoy as a result of the efforts on their behalf of this " host of the ship " would probably be shared by the chief steward himself at finding his " human " qualities so highly regarded by his employers.

Many of these American expedients for importing a sense of personality into work are crude devices for exploiting human nature in the interests of commercial gain ; but it is impossible to proclaim what are commonly regarded as the " non-economic " characteristics of an individual to the crowd of public purchasers without at the same time acknowledging to the worker himself their existence and importance, and in so doing an employer is responding to a true human need which no increase of earnings alone could satisfy. " Men now demand status in industry," says Mr. Hodges, " they have arrived at the stage when they say ' we want to be responsible human beings vested with such power in proportion to our place in industry as

[1] *New York Times*, 29th April, 1923.

will enable each of us to feel that he, as a unit, is personally responsible for the conduct of the industry.' " [1]   If men feel like this it is useless to look for social contentment from " profit-sharing " schemes, when often, as a well-known psychologist remarks, " such schemes are merely another name for ' tips ' bestowed on the workers according to the success of their efforts." [2]   Co-partnership, continues Dr. Myers, must be " a co-partnership in intellect and feeling as well as in stocks and shares." [3]

The Socialist movement in England derives much of its strength from the widely held belief that there is nothing much more to be looked for from the existing economic order by the mass of workers, even in times of prosperity, beyond higher wages and shorter hours ; and that a change in status can only be obtained by a radical transformation of the industrial system.   There is no doubt but that the war of 1914–1918 had an influence in this direction, the effect of which is only beginning to be felt.   The improvement in status which millions of men and women underwent on entering the fighting forces, or even when they took up national work of a civil character, or were transferred from private enterprise to State-controlled industry, was an experience which would not have been forgotten even if it had not been driven home by the official

[1] *Nationalization of the Mines*, by F. Hodges, p. 110.
[2] *Mind and Work*, by C. S. Myers, p. 152.
[3] Ib., p. 154.

propaganda which endeavoured, by emphasizing the change, to induce people to make just such transferences. The fact that the improvement in status was due in part to an abnormal change in national standards of value, which became better in some respects and worse in others, does not affect the argument. The heightened status was often accompanied, especially in the case of men entering the Army and the Navy, by a reduction in money or real income. In England, during the war, the status of soldiers, sailors, statesmen, munition workers, civil servants and, indeed, of everyone who was working for the national purpose of winning the war, was heightened on the one hand ; while on the other hand the process of private profit-making was abused and decried and condemned as " profiteering," and the status of persons engaged in it was perceptibly lowered. Labour leaders in England, especially since the war, have placed before the nation an economic philosophy and an industrial scheme in which the social significance of the worker is stressed in a manner which is in some ways reminiscent of the war-time Government appeals. The rapid growth of the labour movement appears to show that unless the older political parties can find an alternative method of appealing to the desire for status in regard to work, the growing stream of men and women who are transferring their allegiance to a movement where this element of welfare is emphasized is likely to continue to an indefinite extent.

The opponents of the labour movement would do well to consider how slender is the relationship between status and income if they wish to understand why the once powerful watchwords of more output, shorter hours and higher wages no longer produce their wonted effect on great masses of workers in England. Mr. J. A. Hobson may appear somewhat abstract and idealistic to the average business man when he declares that " spirited workers will no longer put up with the encroachments upon their humanity which habit and economic necessity formerly induced them to accept " ; [1] but Lord Haldane was stating a simple fact which cannot be evaded when he said in evidence before the Royal Commission on the Coal Mines that "your General in the Army, your Colonel, your Captain, your Admiral in the Navy, your Commander, live on what the rich man often calls very little indeed, but their reward comes to them in another way. They have social advantages which he has not." [2]

The farther we push the analysis, the more clearly do we find that status is inseparably bound up, not with the income of an individual, not even with the nature of his work, but with its purpose. If we enquire why it is that on the whole the status of

[1] *Incentives in the New Industrial Order*, by J. A. Hobson, p. 32.
[2] *The Problem of Nationalization*, by Lord Haldane, p. 43.

110

soldiers, sailors, civil servants, explorers, artists, lawyers, doctors, teachers, ministers of religion, authors, statesmen, scientists, civil engineers, and so forth is, in varying degrees, usually higher in England than that of the great mass of persons engaged in industrial and commercial processes, it is difficult to resist the conclusion that the main reason is because the work of the former is commonly regarded as possessing a social significance, and aiming at the performance of a social service, beyond the gain of the individual engaged upon it and independent of the size of his or her income.[1]

At first sight this may appear an untenable assertion; for it is quite obvious that the work of the trader and the manufacturer are of essential importance to the community, and that society indeed could dispense with the services of all the professional workers in the world more easily than with the one department of commerce that is engaged in distributing food. The factor which determines the status of the worker, however, is not the actual need of the community for the commodity or service which he produces, but the motive which it is believed serves as an incentive for

[1] Mr. Tawney defines a profession as " a trade which is organized, incompletely, no doubt, but genuinely, for the performance of function. It is not simply a collection of individuals who get a living for themselves by the same kind of work. Nor is it merely a group which is organized exclusively for the protection of its members, though that is normally among its purposes."—*The Acquisitive Society*, p. 106.

111

its production. The professional worker of the type to which reference has been made is assumed to be aware of, and to be motivated by, the social significance of his work; and it is presumed that if occasion arises he will place the fulfilment of that social purpose before his own personal gain. In the case of ordinary business enterprise, on the other hand, the conscious motive of the undertaker or *entrepreneur* is taken to be the making of private profit. The social importance of his work is incidental, arising as it were not from a conscious effort on his part, but as a result of the working of what Adam Smith called the " invisible hand," by which he is led " to promote an end which was no part of his intention." [1] His working days are held to be spent in a continual striving after personal monetary gain; and, providing he does not infringe the criminal code or " the custom of the trade," there is no limit to the extent to which it is regarded as proper for him to exploit the economic possibilities of the situation for his own benefit. Furthermore, his standing as a man of business is determined by the size of his income, and is unaffected by whether he follows a line of prime importance, such as the grain trade, or is concerned with one of the luxury trades of less social importance. Insofar as he is influenced by a consciousness of the social purpose of his work, this influence will tend to modify his acquisitive or self-

[1] *The Wealth of Nations*, edited by E. Cannan, vol. i. p. 421.

112

regarding instinct. It is no exaggeration to say that the more " public spirited " a man is in regard to his business, the more he becomes aware, that is to say, of the social purpose that he serves, and of the importance of this purpose as an element of welfare in his life, the smaller his earnings are likely to be.

The vast majority of men and women engaged in industry and commerce are placed, however, in subordinate positions in which they are powerless to determine how far, if at all, the normal motive of profit seeking which regulates the conduct of private enterprise is to be tempered, in their particular business, by considerations relative to the social purpose which it is the function of that business to fulfil. It is only the exceptionally fortunate worker of whom it is not true that " his daily life is dealt with as a means to another's end " [1] who can, that is, pursue a purpose in his work beyond enriching himself, his employer, or the shareholders of a company. Chamelionlike, he must take on the colour of those for whom he works ; and there is a tragic quality in the quite common occurrence of sensitive and well-intentioned men and women being driven by circumstances to earn their living by working for ends which are in conflict with their " private " beliefs or aspirations.

" The difference," says Mr. Tawney, " between industry as it exists to-day and a profession is simple

[1] *The Decay of Capitalist Civilization*, by S. and B. Webb, p. 48.

and unmistakable. . . . The essence of the one is that
its only criterion is the financial return which it offers
to its shareholders. The essence of the other, is that,
though men enter it for the sake of a livelihood, the
measure of their success is the service which they
perform, and not the gains which they amass. They
may . . . grow rich ; but the meaning of their profession, both for themselves and for the public, is not
that they make money, but that they make health, or
safety, or knowledge, or good government or good
laws. They depend on it for their income, but they
do not consider that any conduct which increases their
income is on that account right." [1] It is an almost
unconscious recognition of the overwhelming predominance of the economic motive in the transactions of
private enterprise which detracts from the status of
those engaged in it, and places them in this respect
in a lower position than public servants and members
of most of the professions. This is not to say that all
commercial and industrial workers are selfish mater-
ialists, and that all doctors and municipal officials and
so forth are altruistic idealists devoid of mercenary
instincts. No one who has lived in the world of men
and observed human nature would postulate that
mankind could be divided on such a basis. But it is
nevertheless true that in most of the professional occupations to which we have referred there is a considerable

The Acquisitive Society, by R. H. Tawney, p. 108.

realm where it is a written or unwritten law that the motive of economic self-interest must be definitely subordinated to considerations of social purpose or the public welfare in a way which does not apply in private enterprise. A doctor may be somewhat unscrupulous in paying unnecessary visits to his patients; but if there is an epidemic of influenza or smallpox he will not raise his fees in order to profit out of the increased demand for his services; yet if the epidemic results in excessive mortality textile manufacturers will not hesitate to raise the price of black mourning fabrics. If a physician discovered the cause and cure for cancer the public would be scandalized if he attempted to exploit his discovery as a private monopoly in the ordinary commercial way. A General who cabled to the War Office refusing to withdraw his troops from a dangerous position or to proceed with a battle unless assured of additional pay would be hounded from the army. An author or an artist who produces work of a low quality for the sake of increasing his income is said to " pot-boil " and his status is lowered thereby; yet few business men will hesitate to produce goods of an inferior quality if it is financially profitable to do so.

It is difficult not to feel that there is something confused in the common social outlook of our time when it applies one conception to certain kinds of work which are termed " professional," and a different conception to certain other kinds of work, of no less value to the community, which come under the heading of commerce and industry. One disadvantage of such a differentiation is that it deprives a vast mass of men and women of the satisfaction which comes to an individual from a conscious belief in, and a widespread recognition of, the social utility of the work which he performs. One of the conditions of happiness, writes Professor Hobhouse, "is that our life should be anchored in some object that takes us beyond ourselves, be that object another person, or our work, or the life of the community . ," [1] and Mr. Hobson goes so far as to say that " a man who is not interested in his work and does not recognize in it either beauty or utility, is degraded by that work, whether he knows it or not." [2] It is certainly true that a man's belief that he is contributing to a conscious effort to enrich the life of the community, or maintain the existing good in it, is, together with the status which is usually enjoyed by those who are recognized as helping to effect that purpose, one of the fundamental elements in the welfare of the individual. More than anything else does it lend him significance in society, and it is this which distinguishes the artist, the statesman, the scientist, and the other acknowledged " servants of mankind " from all who seek merely their own ends.

[1] *The Elements of Social Justice*, by L. T. Hobhouse, p. 18.
[2] *Work and Wealth*, by J. A. Hobson, p. 88.

116

WORK

All these workers feel that they are making an effort to achieve something beyond their own good ; and, whether mistaken or not, they derive from that feeling an irreplaceable and essential element of the good life—but one which is almost unrelated to private income.

A vast increase of human well-being would result both to the individual and to society if we were to think about work less in terms of money or the real income of the economists and more in terms of social purpose and the status of the worker.

A great deal of necessary work appears to most people to be at present unavoidably monotonous and disagreeable ; and thus in any case it will for long remain true, as Mr. Muscio remarks, that " the incentives to much modern industrial work are certainly not exclusively the feelings of pleasure derived from the mere performance of it." [1] Under these circumstances, he continues, work is carried on because of incentives extraneous to the work itself. " In so far as the tendencies excited by these incentives are being realized through the continuance of the work, the feeling tone to the worker will be to some degree pleasurable, and thus will contribute to the further continuance of the work." [2] Monotonous and disagreeable work is to be found in abundance in the professions as well as in

[1] " Feeling Tone in Industry," by B. Muscio, *British Journal of Psychology*, gen. sec. xii. part 2, October 1921.
[2] Ib., p. 162.

industrial occupations; but the feeling tone of a hardworked hospital nurse, motivated more and more, as her term of duty approaches its end, by the extraneous incentive of the purpose and utility of her work, and less and less by the pleasure derived from the work itself, is likely to be more agreeable than the feeling tone of a shorthand typist working overtime who is almost entirely motivated by the extraneous incentive of wanting to augment her salary. It would appear certain, indeed, that the marginal utility of the money-getting incentive by itself as an aid to pleasurable feeling tone is lower and decreases more rapidly than when it is combined with the incentive of social purpose; and possibly it is lower even than the latter operating alone. This is perhaps a somewhat complicated way of saying that *ceteris paribus* a person gets less easily tired and depressed by doing disagreeable work for a purpose which he regards as being socially valuable than if he is doing it only for the purpose of earning money. Whether this is true universally or in certain cases only it is not at present possible to say, but the experience of the war showed that the feeling tone of very large numbers of British soldiers engaged for long periods upon exceptionally monotonous and arduous work remained distinctly higher than the level obtaining in civil life for work of an approximately similar character. Yet the income of the majority of non-commissioned soldiers enlisted temporarily during the war was lower than their normal earnings in civil life.

Considerations of this kind lend force to Mr. Muscio's suggestion that " feelings generally—and not merely ' fatigue ' feelings—should be accorded more notice in connexion with various sides of industrial life than they at present receive." [1]   It can be seen, too, that when Mr. Hodges says that the coalminer " wants to know the social purpose of his work " [2] he is not referring to a form of satisfaction which must inevitably be confined to the few who initiate and organize and discover and create and lead, but to one which may be within the reach also of the many who follow and toil and sweat at even the hardest manual tasks.   For, as Mr. Tawney remarks, when men give the purpose of industry the first place in their thoughts about it, " when their minds are set upon the fact that the meaning of industry is the service of man, all who labour appear to them honourable, because all who labour serve." [3]

We do not at present in England fully realize the value of this feeling of social purpose in regard to work, both as a cause making for industrial efficiency and increased co-operation, and as an element in the well-being of the individual.   In the United States, despite a much more ruthless and ubiquitous economic individualism than exists in Great Britain, there is to be

[1] "Feeling Tone in Industry," by B. Muscio, *British Journal of Psychology*, gen. sec. xii. part 2, October 1921, p. 162,

[2] *Nationalization of the Mines*, by F. Hodges, p. 111.

[3] *The Acquisitive Society*, p. 38.

found a widespread attempt to make enterprises run for private profit simulate the appearance of undertakings carried on primarily or exclusively for the public weal, in a manner which suggests the revival of Adam Smith's " invisible hand " in a new form. No observant visitor to America can fail to be struck by the frequent use in the economic sphere of the word " service," which has about it a flavour of unselfish effort in the interest of others. A typical example of the way in which many large corporations strive to import an atmosphere suggestive of an exclusive devotion to the good of the public is an advertisement which appeared in the *Literary Digest* of 17th March, 1923. Below a pictorial representation of a man working a switchboard in a room filled with water nearly up to his waist, was a description entitled " Why they stick." " It was night," we read, " flood had come upon the city ; death and disaster threatened the inhabitants. Outside the telephone building people had long since sought refuge ; the water mounted higher and higher ; fire broke out. . . . But still the man at the test board stuck to his post, . . . forgetful of self ; thinking only of the needs of the emergency." On a higher floor of the same building, the advertisement continues, a corps of telephone operators worked all through the night in the face of extreme danger. Then follows an explanatory paragraph. " It was the spirit of service that kept them at their work—a spirit beyond thought of advancement or reward. . . . By the nature of telephone service this is the everyday spirit of the Bell System." This spirit, the announcement proceeds, animates every man and woman in the service, whether working "in quiet laboratories or at desks," or on the "highways of speech." They all know, it concludes, "how the safe and orderly life of the people depends on the System—and all know that the System depends on them." At the foot of this advertisement, which unfortunately omits to state not only the name of the city where these heroic feats are said to have taken place, but also the date, and the names of the gallant operators concerned, appears the title of the corporation, its trade mark, and the words, "One policy, one system, Universal Service, and all directed toward Better Service."

An unqualified declaration of this kind of the sovereign predominance of the public good is not in the final analysis compatible with the principles of economic self-interest, particularly in the case of a monopoly, or partial monopoly, such as a telephone undertaking. But the employees of the Corporation, at any rate, are likely to derive more satisfaction from their work than they would if this "public service" aspect of the undertaking received no attention.

In the United States the stressing of this aspect of business is not always a mere device for securing special efforts from employees, or an acquiescence by the public in monopoly. It arises at times from a real conviction on the part of captains of industry regarding the social value of their work. Henry Ford, who is commonly believed to be the richest man in America, writes that " It has been thought that business existed for profit. That is wrong. Business exists for service; it is a profession, and must have recognized professional ethics, to violate which declasses a man." [1] And it is clear from this and the following passage that he not only distinguishes the status and social utility arising from a man's work from the private income which he earns thereby, but also that he values the former very much more than the latter. " We are growing out of this worship of material possessions," he says. " It is no longer a distinction to be rich. As a matter of fact to be rich is no longer a common ambition. It takes only a moment's thought to see that as far as individual personal advantage is concerned, vast accumulations of money mean nothing. . . . But if one has visions of service, if one has vast plans which no ordinary resources could possibly realize, if one has a life ambition to make the industrial desert bloom like a rose, and the workaday life suddenly blossom into fresh and enthusiastic efficiency, then one sees in large sums of money what the farmer sees in his seed corn— the beginning of richer harvests whose benefits can no more be selfishly confined than can the sun's rays." [2]

[1] *My Life and Work*, by Henry Ford, p. 270.   [2] Ib., pp. 268-9.

WORK

It is difficult not to feel, after reading the *Apologia pro sua vita* of an industrial genius like Mr. Ford—despite his declaration on an earlier page that " there is altogether too much reliance on good feeling in our business organizations "—that Mr. J. A. Hobson is right in at least one case when he remarks that " rents of ability, as well as of superior opportunity, are often taken by industrialists, merchants and professional men, far exceeding the necessary incentives to evoke the use of their special ability." [1]

It may not be possible to agree with Mr. Ford as to the impossibility of restricting economic benefits, or as to the certainty of their inevitable diffusion in a manner as impartial as the rays of the sun. But his statement is significant as one of many indications that certain American business men have come to feel that the satisfaction to be derived from economic activities, when regarded merely as methods of making money for themselves, is inadequate ; and that they are seeking more and more to conceive their work in terms of social purpose.

But side by side with this phenomenon there is to be observed in the United States a disposition on the part of public servants to regard their work chiefly from the point of view of the personal gain to themselves, in a manner which reminds one of the corrupt patronage system in eighteenth century England. Mr. John D.

[1] *Incentives in the New Social Order*, by J. A. Hobson, p. 38.

Nagle, for example, who was recently appointed Immigration Commissioner for the port of San Francisco, is reported to have said, when notified of his nomination, " That is good news to me. While it has seemed a long while to my friends, I was always confident that Senators Johnson and Shortridge and my strong political friends here and elsewhere, were always looking after my interests." [1] The disadvantages attaching to this attitude affect not only the public welfare, but also the official himself. No man can obtain the satisfaction which comes from a belief in the public utility of his work if his first thought in connexion with that work is his own " interests " ; and yet that satisfaction is one of the essential elements of his well-being. Lord Haldane, in answer to a question addressed to him before the Royal Commission which was considering the Nationalization of the Coal Mines, said, " I think there are a great many men who would be prepared to serve the State at moderate salaries, if they were to have the prospect of becoming distinguished in the sense of having rank and recognition. I am sure that just as in the Army and Navy you find men ready to go in and take a very small living wage, for the honour and glory of the thing ;

---

[1] *San Francisco Bulletin*, 2nd March, 1923, leading article. In the same newspaper it was announced that Mr. New, who was about to assume office as Postmaster-General in President Harding's cabinet, would revert to the system of regarding appointments in the postal service as political rewards, and would henceforth nominate postmasters throughout the country on that principle.

so you would find it in the Civil Service, if we based
the Civil Service on that foundation." [1] But he had
in mind the tradition and the outlook of the modern
British Civil Service, rather than the point of view
expressed by Mr. Nagle. And in thinking of those
who might be animated by that spirit, he had in mind
those whose welfare in regard to their work is higher,
despite a modest income, than it was in the days when
Mr. Nagle's point of view commonly prevailed in the
public service. "What men of science want," said
Huxley, "is only a fair day's wages for more than a
fair day's work " ; [2] yet he was not thinking of scientists
as self-sacrificing heroes who were doomed by their
vocation to miss the good things of life, but rather as
ordinary men who were exceptionally fortunate in
having "the means of making themselves useful to
their age and generation," and whose own lives were
enriched and brightened by the sense of well-being
which comes from appropriate work performed for a
high end. We cannot all be scientists or original
workers in any field, but we can all obtain pleasure,
satisfaction—even happiness—from our occupation if
we will but look upon our work in a manner similar
to that of all the greatest Workers in every land and
in every age, and reject and replace that part of the
existing economic fabric of society which does not
harmonize with that conception.

[1] *Nationalization of the Mines*, by Lord Haldane, p. 32.
[2] *Critiques and Addresses*, by T. H. Huxley, p. 30.

THE RELATION OF WEALTH TO WELFARE

In summarizing the argument contained in this chapter we can see that the wheel has turned full circle. For its starting point was the assertion that work forms an important element in human welfare ; but that the relation between the work and the worker, as distinct from the question of his real or money earnings, has hitherto received insufficient attention ; with unfortunate results. A correspondence between natural capacity and productive function is, we saw, essential to individual and social welfare, but this correspondence is not at present closely related, with certain exceptions, to private income. In any case the advantages or disadvantages resulting from this relationship cannot be expressed in terms of money. At present the prevailing incidence of opportunity often prevents even well-marked and exceptional talent from finding an appropriate vocational expression ; but a still more widespread form of social waste and ill-fare is caused by the absence of scientific enquiry as to the inherent aptitudes of those who show no well-marked specific capacity. Vocational guidance requires collective action and a considerable readjustment of current ideas. Economic status is another aspect of work which is of definite importance to individual well-being ; but its connexion with income is slight. A close investigation of the nature of status in modern economic life shows the demand for improved status to be based on a desire on the part of the worker to secure the recognition of his whole personality in reference to his work. Status is closely bound up with the existence of a recognition by the worker himself and the society in which he lives of the social purpose, real or assumed, served by his work, and a supposed willingness on his part, often borne out by the facts, to prefer that purpose to his own interests where they conflict. The differentiation in this respect between business and the professional occupations is inexpedient inasmuch as it deprives large numbers of men and women of important forms of satisfaction which cannot be obtained by means of increase of income alone. A belief by an individual in the social utility of his work is of considerable value in itself, both as an incentive and as a reward and also as an aid to a pleasurable " feeling tone " in the actual performance of the work itself. It is an advantage which need not necessarily be confined to those kinds of work which require exceptional gifts. It bears no definite relation to private income.

VARIATIONS ON THE THEME

CHAPTER FIVE

EDUCATION

No analysis comparing the welfare derived from individual enterprise and private income with that springing from collective action and public expenditure could afford to leave education out of account. It is therefore this element of welfare which we shall now discuss.

So far as the growth of education in modern times is concerned, it is not difficult to trace the main source of development. Every western country has adopted a system of public education, paid for and maintained by the nation in its collective capacity ; and to-day such a system of compulsory instruction is generally regarded as constituting one of the essential functions of government in a civilized State. It is an obvious and undeniable fact that most of the great flow of literary education is maintained by public effort and public expenditure, despite a multitude of small and for the most part inefficient private schools in England, and a mass of enormous university endowments in the United States of America. Even the Universities of Oxford and Cambridge, until recently independent of all State aid, could scarcely be termed private enterprises ; and a similar corporate or collective character adheres to the so-called public schools in England, which usually rest on large ancient endowments, or are maintained by one or another of the ancient livery companies.

Whatever may be thought of the results of collective effort in modern times in the sphere of education, it is quite certain that private enterprise, in the ordinary sense of voluntary supply and demand, has been and still is a failure in this connexion. Education has become increasingly an affair of State concern during the past century. Yet in England, at any rate, there was no *a priori* belief that education was one of the legitimate, or essential, or even permissible, duties of the State ; and government accepted the task and assumed financial responsibility by successive steps only as the inability of voluntary agencies and private enterprise to achieve success on an effective scale unaided became apparent. Between 1850 and 1870 real wages and profits rose more rapidly than at any previous time during the century,[1] more rapidly, indeed, than at any time in the whole history of England ; yet even these unprecedented increases of income did not bring mere literacy to the mass of the nation.

By the middle of the nineteenth century a realization of the danger and waste involved by the absence in the vast majority of English men and women of even

[1] Cf. *The Industrial and Commercial Revolutions in Great Britain*, by L. C. A. Knowles, pp. 168–9.

the rudiments of an education became sufficiently widespread to constitute a serious movement for public intervention. The opposition to State interference was based on several arguments, of which the religious proved ultimately the most controversial and persistently obstructive. But, from the first, one of the main objections arose from the identification of social welfare with private income and the rights of property. " Our definition of State-duty forbids the State . . . to administer education," wrote Herbert Spencer in 1850, " inasmuch as the taking away of his [a citizen's] property to educate his own or other people's children is not needful for the maintaining of his rights ; the taking away of his property for such a purpose is wrong." [1] Few people would oppose public educational activities to-day with arguments concerning the abstract right or wrong of the matter considered in the light of " State-duty "; yet the opposition to the " taking away of property " for the purpose of education continues unabated. The chief difference is that the argument is in our own time based either on a postulated need for economy in national expenditure, or on the alleged inability of public education to enhance the welfare of the nation. Change the one word " rights " to " welfare," and the passage from Spencer quoted above might be taken from a current issue of a Conservative newspaper.

[1] *Social Statics*, by H. Spencer, p. 82

EDUCATION

The habit of identifying welfare with private income and private expenditure has not only hindered the development of our educational system, but has also prevented a just appreciation of what it has already achieved. Because educational activities do not produce a traceable financial result which can be compared quantitatively with its cost the better-off classes of the community have often felt, or pretended to feel, sceptical as to the benefits accrueing from public expenditure on that service. Moreover, a temperamental disinclination to admit that positive welfare could result from collective activities in any sphere save those of military conquest and defence, and civil justice, has led to an underrating of just those benefits which are valued most highly when arising from the private expenditure of parents upon their children. If it could have been demonstrated that every £1,000 spent annually on national education brought an increase in the national dividend of £1,100 ; or that every £100 per annum invested in a youth through the national schools yielded eventually a certain return to him of £150 a year more than he would otherwise have earned, public expenditure on education would no doubt have been considered fully justified, and its progressive expansion assured. But although it is quite conceivable that results of this kind may actually occur, it is not possible in the present state of social science to bring the fruits of educational expenditure

131

into direct relation with "the measuring rod of money." Hence many arguments in recent years have been advanced with the object of holding up public education as an extravagance. The committee of wealthy business men appointed by the Government in 1922 to consider national expenditure, and presided over by Sir Eric Geddes, made no effort whatever to evaluate the worth of education either in the life of the individual or of the community, but proceeded without delay to recommend "reducing the expenditure on elementary education . . . by raising the lower age limit, by putting more pupils under one teacher, and paying the teachers less." [1] In regard to higher education, financial considerations were again isolated and attention concentrated exclusively upon them. "Every effort should be made to reduce the cost of secondary education," [2] the report runs; and, "as regards Higher Education generally and Scholarships, the expenditure is in excess of the nation's ability to pay, and must be reduced." [3] In another place the Committee says that "if the standard of staffing were raised in urban areas so that there were in future one teacher to each fifty pupils, the saving would be £8,282,000, of which £4,853,000 would accrue to the taxpayer." [4]

There is to be observed in these passages in the first

[1] Report of Geddes Committee on National Expenditure, Cd. 1581/1922, p. 111.
[2] Ib., p. 114.   [3] Ib., p. 122.   [4] Ib., p. 110.

place an assumed identification of private income with welfare, and in the second place an implied belief that money diverted from private possession to public expenditure upon education is a process inevitably impoverishing to the individual and to the community. Without some kind of a conception as to the objects of education, and some agreement as to the desirability of attaining those objects, it is not altogether clear what is meant by the recommendation that " every effort " should be made to reduce the cost of secondary education. It might mean the entire abolition of secondary schools, or it might mean their curtailment in numbers and quality to an extent compatible with the achievement of certain results. But those results cannot be defined in terms of money. The phrase " ability to pay " is, again, not free from intellectual confusion in so far as it identifies economic possibility with the opinion of the Committee as to what is socially desirable. In 1921 the expenditure of the inhabitants of Great Britain upon alcoholic liquor was estimated at four hundred million pounds ; and in 1922 at over three hundred and fifty millions— about five times as much as the total expenditure upon national education. But it would be absurd to say unconditionally that this amount was in excess of the nation's ability to pay. All that could properly be said is that a disbursement on this scale is incompatible with the attainment of certain results which may or may not be considered desirable. The manufacture and sale of spirituous liquor is highly profitable, in terms of money, to all concerned. The brewer and the publican make a large profit, the Government draws a large tax, and the consumer obtains a commodity of a tangible nature which he can measure. But a conclusion as to the advantageousness of this expenditure upon intoxicating drink could not be reached merely by considering its effects on the private incomes of those who produce and those who consume alcoholic liquor. Certain other aspects of individual and national life would have to be taken into account. It would be necessary, for example, to note, among other things, the fact that there was an increase in the number of persons charged with drunkenness from 75,859 in 1857 (3·94 per thousand of the population) to 183,221 in 1885 (6·73 per thousand) and 210,024 in 1907 (6·01 per thousand); [1] followed by a reduction for the years 1916–1920 to an average of 66,220 (1·97 per thousand).[2] It would be necessary to consider the scientific evidence which enabled the Chief Medical Officer of Health to observe that "an habitual excessive consumption of alcohol does definite harm to the body, and, other things being equal, nations which drink alcohol to excess cannot compete on equal physical terms with nations which are moderate or

[1] *Public Health and Social Conditions* (statistical memoranda prepared in the Local Government Board), Cd. 4671/1909, p. 109
[2] *Judicial Statistics*, part i. 1920, p. 14.

abstaining in this respect " ; [1] and an investigation would have to be made as to how far the need for lunatic asylums, workhouses, prisons and poor relief is directly occasioned by the liquor traffic. Alternative methods of raising revenue ; the effect of the consumption of alcohol upon the consumption of sugar ; and the relation of individual freedom to law-breaking and law enforcement would, in addition to various other aspects of the subject, have to be considered before an acceptible conclusion could be formulated as to the effect on the welfare of the nation of this expenditure on alcoholic drink.

A similar treatment is required in regard to education, if any useful estimate is to be arrived at concerning the effect on welfare of public expenditure on this service. It is true, as Mr. Philip Wicksteed observes in connexion with the general difficulty of testing high social aims quantitatively, that " the rule seems to hold that the higher and more ideal your purpose, the greater your difficulty in gaining any assurance that you have accomplished it." [2] But although the results of education cannot be brought into direct relation with its cost, there are nevertheless some definite aspects of the matter which deserve attention.

The annual cost of the system of national education has risen from less than a million pounds in 1865 [3] to

[1] *On the State of the Public Health*, 1921, p. 87.
[2] *The Common Sense of Political Economy*, p. 676.
[3] The total cost in 1865 was probably about £3,000,000.

seventy-seven millions in 1921. One result has been to wipe out almost entirely the widespread illiteracy which prevailed in this country up to nearly the end of last century. So late as 1865, in every thousand couples married in England and Wales, no less than 225 men and 312 women were unable even to sign their names in the register. By 1907 the numbers had fallen to 14 and 17 respectively.[1] Thus the machinery of literary intercourse has been created ; and the accomplishments of reading and writing, for centuries during the middle ages the almost exclusive possession of the Church, have been thrown open to the great mass of men and women. Some of the uses to which these accomplishments are put makes them a not unmixed blessing ; but men and women to-day keep in touch with thoughts and events in a world vastly larger than that in which their forefathers lived. The entry of millions of men and women into clerical occupations, or those incidentally requiring a knowledge of reading, writing and arithmetic, has made possible the enormous expansion of the distributive trades upon which economic inter-dependence and organized co-operation depend.[2]

The connexion between crime and education is

[1] *Public Health and Social Conditions*, Cd. 4671/1909, p. 102.
[2] In our present badly organized society there often exists an unnecessary multiplication of distributive processes which is costly and wasteful. But this is due to a mere perversion. There is to-day at once both too much and too little organized distribution.

known to be a fairly close one, and an examination of the criminal statistics during the past three-quarters of a century is not without interest. The following table shows the number of persons annually tried in England and Wales for indictable offences, which comprises murder and other offences against the person, offences against property (with or without violence), larcenies, forgery, and other crimes of a serious order. Larceny accounts for about five-sixths of the aggregate.

Year.	Number.	Per Thousand of Population.	Index Number.
1857	84,667	2·84	100
1865	59,886	2·83	100
1875	49,996	2·08	74
1885	56,437	2·07	73
1895	50,518	1·67	59
1905	61,463	1·80	64
1906–10	64,423	1·83	64
1911–15	61,442	1·67	59
1916–20	58,830	1·75	62

Taking into account the considerable increase in the size and efficiency of the police force within the last half century, these figures, in the words of an official report, " may fairly be taken as evidence of a real decrease in crime." [1]   It is impossible not to recognize

[1] *Public Health and Social Conditions*, p. 103.   The figures are taken partly from p. 109 of the same blue book, and partly from *Judicial Statistics*, part i, *Criminal Statistics*, 1922, p. 13.

that one important cause of this unprecedented diminution in the most serious class of criminal offence has been the spread of education. The first Act of Parliament establishing the foundation of the national system was passed in 1870 ; but considerable grants to voluntary societies in aid of schools had been made from 1847 onwards.

One of the unique features of the war of 1914–18 was the gradual realization, for the first time in the history of the British Army, of the military value of education, not merely in the case of the commissioned officer, but for all ranks. An elaborate organization was set up in 1918, at the very climax of the war, to provide educational opportunities of a cultural nature for men in training and those in the camps and depôts behind the lines in France and elsewhere. The view taken by the authorities at the War Office is set forth in certain official publications which were issued with Army Orders. " Educational training," commanding officers were told, " is not to be regarded as a secondary consideration, nor for spare hours as a form of recreation ; but as an essential element in the making of a soldier and an army." The considerations upon which this " principle " was based were that " The real difficulty of the battle training of the modern soldier render it necessary that he should be quick, intelligent and, as far as possible of a ready understanding. . . . Further, it is demanded nowadays that a man should understand what he is being taught, and the reasons for his instruction ; he must not merely learn by rule of thumb."[1] Nor was this all. Importance was attached to " the bearing of educational training upon morale." Nothing could be further from the tradi- tional conception of the soldier's duty : " Theirs not to reason why, theirs but to do and die." It is certain that such a revolutionary change in the outlook of the highest military authorities, opposed as it was to all the traditional tendencies of the British War Office, and involving a divergence of human energy and organization at a moment when there was a critical shortage of man power, could only have been induced by the irrefragable logic of experience. So long as the lack of international co-operation continues to result in the maintenance of military forces, it is desirable in the national interest that those forces should be efficient from a military point of view, and of a reliable morale. The relation of national education to national security in a warring world is a matter which merits attention, as well as the development of a more pacific spirit for the settlement of disputes by the same social instrument. At the same time it appears probable that an army of educated citizens would prove more likely to require persuasion, and be more difficult to persuade, of the so-called righteousness and alleged

[1] *Educational Training.* Issued with Army Order VII, dated 13th May, 1919, p. 1. This superseded several earlier pamphlets of a similar nature.

moral validity of the cause in support of which it might be asked to fight, than would an army of uneducated men.

The utility of education in reference to commerce and industry has become widely recognized during the past five and twenty years. Up to about the middle of last century, although the wealthy class was almost entirely composed of those persons who had received what was then regarded as a liberal education, the common notion prevailed that education was inevitably the result of wealth rather than its cause ; and under the conditions then existing this was not untrue. The rise of the modern cities in the north of England based on the new and rapidly expanding textile and engineering and mining industries, enabled many unlettered men of humble origin to make large fortunes as the industrial revolution quickened its pace. But these self-made capitalists took pride in their very lack of educational training, inasmuch as it seemed to lend additional merit to their business achievements ; and hence there was no emphasis laid on the advantages of education in industry or commerce, or on the need for it as a means of providing opportunity in the economic sphere.

As the nineteenth century drew to a close, however, the growing competition of German industry weakened the belief that all the skill and organizing ability, all the enterprise and inventive genius required by British industry would be automatically provided by the inevitable emergence of individuals gifted by nature with these qualities. The Education Act of 1870 had only established elementary schools; and "almost every year," to quote Dr. Marshall, "brought new evidence that a niggardly policy of education was a mistake even from a purely commercial point of view."[1] It was becoming increasingly clear that the industrial revolution had passed into a new phase, in which the kind of new discovery and invention which was now needed did not come to men without scientific training, by strokes of sudden inspiration, as had previously often been the case. The age called, as Marshall says, for " a new class of improvements of method, and —in a less degree—for improvements of appliances, which cannot be created by a single alert individual," but which are " the product of sustained researches by large groups of specially qualified students extending over a period of time."[2]

The bulk of these sustained researches took place, in the thirty years before the war of 1914, in Germany; and the challenge of German competition was in consequence becoming increasingly disadvantageous to British industry. Despite a vague uneasiness and a feeling that " something ought to be done " there was no clear conviction that a greatly increased public expenditure on national education might " pay " in

[1] *Industry and Trade*, by A. Marshall, p. 98.   [2] Ib., p. 97.

terms of industrial progress ; and the war knocked the bottom out of the German argument before the lesson had been driven home.

One of the striking features of the post-war world is the strong economic rivalry which is developing between England and the United States of America. In that competition Great Britain is handicapped from competing on equal terms by several severe disadvantages, one of which is the inadequate educational equipment of her men of business. Mr. Graham Wallas, writing in 1921, remarked that " an Englishman in the United States envies the universal recognition of education as desirable, and the open-handed generosity both of public grants and private gifts to every kind of educational institution. The United States, with rather more than twice the population of the United Kingdom, has more than four times as many students in secondary schools, and more than eight times in Universities." [1] Mr. J. A. Hobson, speaking as an economist of the " lack of trained ability in the applied sciences, in finance, and in business administration " in England, refers to the monetary " undervaluation of what we may call her brain-capital in favour of material capital." [2] This is largely due, he adds, to " the comparative intellectual ease with which the fabric of British capitalism has been built up."

[1] *Our Social Heritage*, p. 50.
[2] *Incentives in the New Industrial Order*, p. 63.

142

EDUCATION

Evidence as to the value of education in the economic life of the nation is overwhelming, despite the impossibility of measuring the results in exact terms of money. Sir Robert Waley Cohen, one of the directors of the great Asiatic Petroleum Company, giving evidence before the Royal Commission on the Civil Service on behalf of his firm, said : " We started employing them [university men from Cambridge] in 1907. At that time our business began to expand extremely rapidly, and we found ourselves in the need of men capable of managing and handling other men, men of initiative and tact, capable of grasping new situations, and generally men possessed of all the qualities of character and intelligence and mental development which are required for occupying important posts in a business. . . . At that time we took into our business in one of these positions a university man from another business, and we were very much struck at once with the consequences of it." In reply to another question Mr. Waley Cohen (as he then was) continued : " We took more and more of such men, and in the course of the five years which have elapsed since then we have taken forty-one men from Cambridge for the general part of our business, and five scientific men for the technical side of the business." [1] The same conclusion is reached without a single exception by the leading

[1] MacDonnell Commission on the Civil Service, Appendix to 3rd Report, Minutes of Evidence, Q.21524/5, p. 257, 1913, Cd. 6720.

economists of the day. Professor Marshall is only voicing the general consensus of opinion when he remarks that " there is no extravagance more prejudicial to the growth of national wealth than that wasteful negligence which allows genius that happens to be born of lowly parentage to expend itself in lowly work. No change would conduce so much to a rapid increase of material wealth as an improvement in our schools, and especially those of the middle grades, provided it be combined with an extensive system of scholarships which will enable the clever son of a working man to rise gradually from school to school till he has the best theoretical and practical education which the age can give." [1] In another place he says that public expenditure on education is profitable as a mere investment, and that " the economic value of one great industrial genius is sufficient to cover the expenses of the education of a whole town." [2] In a more recent volume he points out that one of the ways in which education can assist industry is by securing properly trained diplomatic and consular services, for every country can be helped or hindered industrially by the excellence or feebleness of the information regarding economic questions and trade opportunities obtained by its foreign emissaries. " With a few brilliant exceptions," he adds, " British Consuls seem to have

[1] *Principles of Economics*, p. 12
[2] Ib., p. 216.

144

lagged far behind those of America and Germany in such matters." [1]

In none of his remarks advocating an extension of public educational activities does Professor Marshall step outside the economic sphere : all his recommendations, it will be noted, are based on what is desirable merely from the point of view of increasing material wealth. In a similar way it is possible to assert the advantageousness of a greater equality of opportunity on purely economic grounds. Huxley said long ago that education was the instrument by which " men of brass " could be picked out from the men of silver and gold and placed on that rung in the economic ladder to which they were by nature suited. [2] And Dr. Dalton, in a recent book, observes that " The general effect of improved education would be to increase what has been called ' Vertical mobility ' in the sense of the mobility of the workers from the worse paid to the better paid occupations." [3] It would appear that the desirability of putting into operation all measures, educational or otherwise, likely to bring about a greater equality of opportunity in the economic sphere must be admitted with special emphasis by those who think it best that the existing industrial and commercial system should continue virtually

[1] *Industry and Trade*, p. 102.

[2] " Administrative Nihilism," in *Critiques and Addresses*, by T. H. Huxley, p. 6.

[3] *The Inequality of Incomes*, by H. Dalton, p. 267.

unchanged. For that system is everywhere defended, where it is defended, on the grounds that it leaves each man free to rise or fall according to his capabilities. That is to say, those who support the existing order presume that equality of opportunity does actually prevail ; and they can therefore hardly oppose measures devised to remedy such inequalities as can be shown in fact to exist.

It might seem unnecessary, or at least platitudinous, to refer to the value of education from a political point of view. It might be thought that the advantages of public educational activities would be recognized, in any country where a democratic system of political government was in operation, on the grounds of the necessity for creating a measure of political enlightenment in the mass of the electorate. Yet such a recognition does not exist ; and a word must therefore be said concerning this aspect of the matter. Just over fifty years ago Thomas Huxley, in a passage which forms one of the most remarkable prophecies in the whole history of social thought, asked, " What now gives force to the Socialistic movement which is now stirring European society to its depths, but a determination on the part of the naturally able men among the proletariat, to put an end, somehow or other, to the misery and degradation in which a large proportion of their fellows are steeped ? The question, whether the means by which they propose to achieve this end are adequate or not . . . is beside my present purpose to discuss. All I desire to point out is, that if the chance of the controversy being decided calmly and rationally, and not by passion and force, looks miserably small to an impartial by-stander, the reason is that not one in ten thousand of those who constitute the ultimate court of appeal . . . is prepared by education to comprehend the real nature of the suit brought before their tribunal." [1]

Thus wrote Huxley in 1871, seven years after the founding of the First Socialist International. The preceding year, 1870, had seen the passing of the first Education Act in England, under which the School Boards were to be set up and the Board Schools subsequently erected and maintained. In the fifty years which have passed since then the growth of public education has been continuous, both in England and on the continent of Europe. But the spread of a belief in various forms of Socialism has been far more rapid still ; and Huxley's analysis of the cause, and his pessimistic prophecy as to the methods likely to prevail must appear more challenging and ominous to the present generation, which has witnessed a whole series of convulsive events in Russia, Hungary, Italy, Spain and Germany, a constitutional revolution of far-reaching importance in England, and an era of extreme violence and intolerance in the United States, than

[1] T. H. Huxley, op. cit., p. 10.

they did even to that of his own day. It is difficult in the post-war world, looking at the actual sequence of political facts at home and abroad, not to feel that there is a widespread conflict going on between the violence incited by inflamed passions on the one hand, and the voice of Reason on the other. In many of the great questions of the day Reason appears definitely to be getting the worst of it, to be outstripped in the race, whether we turn to the activities of the Left, or to those of the Right. And since education consists largely in leading the individual towards the life of Reason, and enabling him to listen and understand and respond to the dictates of her voice, it seems fairly certain that the only effective method of warding off catastrophic political events is by a much more sincere and widespread appreciation of the value of education as an instrument of pacific settlement in public affairs, and a much greater enthusiasm for an extension of public educational activities in every direction than at present exists. Social reformers of every creed and colour are gradually coming to agree that not much progress or improvement of any kind is to be hoped for without educational development, not merely among the manual and clerical workers and the other wage-earning classes, but also, as an imperative necessity, among the better-off sections of society. What is likely to be done or proposed in the future to effect this will be opposed mainly by the argument that national expenditure on education is an act of spending for which no return, or no adequate return, is secured to the individual.

What I have attempted to show here is that a very definite return is actually secured by that form of collective activity and public expenditure; but that it comes not as a specific or traceable item in the money income of the individual, but in the guise of certain forms of welfare. It comes in the shape of a community more law-abiding and less given to crime. It comes in the shape of a people better fitted to defend itself in case of need; more able to embark upon great trading enterprises which take the whole world for their province; more likely to keep in the forefront of scientific discovery and inventive application; more adequately equipped to weather the storm of economic competition (which must inevitably continue to exist in some form under *any* system of production); more likely to decide its political and economic affairs by peaceful means rather than by violence; more open to make full use of differential biological advantages by means of an equitable distribution of human opportunity. Thus, although it is impossible to talk intelligibly about education in terms of money and of monetary income, it is possible and even useful to discuss it in terms of crime, military efficiency, economic expansion, equality of opportunity, scientific invention, civil peace, social contentment, and a number of other things ; and, if such matters are taken into consideration, it will be observed that the individual does in fact receive a return from his contribution to the public expenditure on the education service.

All these aspects are, nevertheless, partial and incomplete fragments of the real justification and the true regard of education, which have their roots in something deeper and more elusive than anything of which mention has been made. The fundamental return which the individual receives from all forms of education worthy of the name is, as has well been said, " the heightened human capacity which they evoke."[1] But that heightening of human capacity, that bringing to fruition of the finest potentialities of human nature, is a process which defies quantitative determination of any kind. Thus we find ourselves here in a world where, in the final analysis, values depend upon intuitive perceptions and upon them alone ; and at this point all argument is unavailing and we shall accordingly carry this part of the discussion no farther.

To recapitulate. Enough has been said concerning the nature of the return yielded by educational activities to enable us to conclude, with Mr. Tawney, that " talk about the cost of education, which ignores the effect of it upon the character and intelligence and

[1] *Secondary Education for All,* edited by R. H. Tawney, p. 63

physical well-being, in the output of industry and the amenity of social life, is as rational as a discussion of one side of a balance sheet without reference to the other." [1] As regards the method by which educational development on a popular scale has been achieved in western countries, it is an obvious fact, as we remarked at the beginning of this chapter, that collective action and public expenditure have in the main been responsible for nearly all that has been done. Wherever a literate nation is to be found, wherever a society is imbued with the rudiments of scientific and historical and literary knowledge, wherever a community is familiar with the background of culture, we find that that result has been brought about by collective action and public expenditure. Yet there is seldom if ever to be found a State monopoly preventing or restricting private enterprise in regard to education. It cannot even be said that the vast predominance of State activities in this field is the inevitable result of the governing authority being able to supply education free, or at less than its cost price, to the poorer classes, by means of taxing the wealthy and subsidizing the public educational service therewith ; for the supremacy of the State as an educator is no greater in countries such as England, where this subsidization does actually take place on a large scale, than it is in

[1] Op. cit., p. 143. On the point of the great influence of national education on physical well-being, see the Report of the Chief Medical Officer, *On the State of the Public Health*, 1923, p. 169

countries such as New Zealand and Scandinavia where a much greater economic egalitarianism prevails, and where the subsidization is inconsiderable. It cannot be said that without the public provision of education as a subsidized service large masses of the community would everywhere be unable to afford to go to school at all ; for in the United States of America, for instance, it can fairly be held that at least every white citizen could afford to pay for his children to be educated at the ordinary economic price.

Looking at the facts impartially, and taking into account what has actually occurred historically, we are entitled to conclude that, for reasons unassigned, private income has been unable to obtain, save in a very small minority of instances, a satisfactory educational service provided by private enterprise. It is immaterial whether this is due to the fact that the mass of parents and guardians have been unable or unwilling to pay for their children's schooling at the profit-making prices required by private enterprise, or to some other reason. The outstanding fact remains that everywhere it has been necessary for collective action and public expenditure to step in and provide the service. Because the benefits which accrue from that public effort are received in kind and do not enter into the money income of those among whom they are distributed, national education is alleged to be a " spending " service ; and held up as an extravagance which a nation that spends more than five times as much on drink is supposed not to be able to afford. Yet the educational institutions which are run for profit, and which are to that extent less economical than the national schools from the social point of view, are neither condemned as extravagant, nor regarded as in any way involving waste.

CHAPTER SIX

CONCORD

WE have now examined at some length certain definite and fundamental elements of human welfare, and considered each of them in turn in relation to private income on the one hand and various kinds of collective action on the other. The four elements thus discussed were Health, Art, Work and Education. The wide diversity in their nature made it necessary to adjust the method of analysis to suit the particular topic under discussion, with the result that the conclusions which have been reached have not the rigorous uniformity of a simple formula.

Despite the individual deviation of particular cases, certain broad conclusions common to all do emerge clearly; and it is with these that we are now concerned. The first is that the power of private income to increase the welfare of its possessor in regard to the various elements under examination is as a matter of fact frequently or even always comparatively small; whereas the power of collective action and public expenditure to do so is often comparatively great. It was seen, for example, that so far as health is concerned, many of the essential conditions of hygiene are beyond

154

the power of purchase by private income, but definitely within the scope of the public medical service, and that others depend on personal activities unrelated to the command of money. In the province of æsthetic experience we found that the individual can with his money neither purchase the ability to appreciate or produce artistic beauty himself, nor stimulate the artist to high creative effort by the same means, whereas under favourable circumstances both results can be and are in fact achieved by social forces exerted by the community as a whole. We observed, again, that the satisfaction which comes from work arises not from the income which is received therefrom, but from the marriage of function and capacity in the worker and a consciousness of the social purpose which he is serving through the performance of it. In the sphere of education we found that most of the development and progress witnessed in recent times has sprung from collective action and public expenditure. These are but a few fragmentary examples of what has been shown by our enquiry in these fields, and for a fuller account we must refer the reader to the foregoing chapters.

We have seen, in the second place, that neither the welfare which a man derives from the enjoyment of some or all of these elements of the good life, nor the deprivation which he suffers when they are absent from his existence, appears normally in any measurable or recognizable way in the sum total of his private income, whether calculated in terms of money or of the so-called " real " income of the economists.

Private income is, of course, of prime and essential importance to an individual as a means of obtaining many of the necessities and decencies and luxuries of life ; and it is clear that one great advantage it possesses as an instrument of distribution is that it enables a person to spend according to his choice, to suit the vagaries of his personal taste, or to refrain from spending at all. I do not for one moment deny the advantages of private monetary income as an economic device of great merit. It would easily be possible to fill many pages with its praises, and to assert the incontrovertible fact that increases or decreases of income do result in definite increases or decreases, whether proportionate or not, of house accommodation, food, clothing and all manner of other articles of consumption ; and that, in consequence, in so far as the welfare of the possessor depends upon a supply, or a larger or better supply, of these and other commodities and services, his welfare is actually enhanced by increases of private income. The merits of private wealth are so widely recognized, however, that it would be merely platitudinous to proclaim the benefits which are conferred by private income on its possessor ; and the object of this book has been to demonstrate instead the limitations of those benefits, and to point out the extent and importance of the spheres of welfare which lie partially or entirely outside the power of purchase by private income. Those spheres are of so essential a nature that we may justifiably conclude that private income is a very bad index to human welfare ; and that an economic system which depends on the assumption that increases or decreases of private income necessarily lead to increases or decreases (whether proportionate or disproportionate) of the welfare of individual possessors of it is based on a fallacious hypothesis as regards several of the most important elements of well-being.

An attempt has been made in the preceding pages to describe the nature and extent of the benefits which are conferred on the individual through the workings of collective action and public expenditure in various spheres of his life where the positive rewards of social effort are usually ignored ; and to suggest at the same time the great potential advantages which further effort in these provinces might produce. It would be absurd to infer that it follows as a result of this that all collective expenditure is necessarily conducive to increased personal welfare, and I do not make that suggestion at all. As Professor Cannan has pointed out, it is quite possible to conceive a socialistic society, for example, which might spend the whole of its surplus income over and above bare necessities on preparations for war ; [1] and we have, indeed, only to turn to the

[1] *The Economic Outlook.*

THE RELATION OF WEALTH TO WELFARE

Report of the Geddes Committee to see how unprofitable and wasteful, so far as human welfare is concerned, much of our national expenditure actually is at present. There we read that " the estimates provide that in the year 1923, the fifth year after the Armistice was signed, with a broken and exhausted Europe, and with no German menace, we are to have far greater fighting power, with a larger personnel, and greater preparations for war than ever before in our history." [1] The question of whether war-like preparations on this scale are or are not necessary if a certain military position is to be maintained is beside the point ; all we are concerned to show here is that much public expenditure often brings little or no positive welfare to the lives of those on whose behalf it is disbursed, and from whose pockets the revenue is collected.

Despite a widespread failure to recognize the positive value of the contribution to welfare made in certain ways by collective effort, public opinion, generally speaking, has moved forward a considerable distance from the extreme individualist point of view epitomized by Herbert Spencer, who, three-quarters of a century ago, went so far as to declare that " one who is rightly constituted cannot be helped. To do anything for him by some artificial agency " [by which he meant the State] " is to supersede certain of his powers—is

[1] First Interim Report of the Committee on National Expenditure, Cd. 1581/1922, p. 7. The increased cost over that of 1914 was then £95,000,000 per annum.

to leave them unexercised, and, therefore, to diminish his happiness." [1] To-day, we get even so able and spirited a defender of the existing economic order as Mr. Hartley Withers admitting that in so far as taxation is " the process by which the State takes money from us . . . to spend on the defence of our property from home or foreign enemies, on the defence of the national honour if need be, on the increase of the material and other resources of the country, and on the public health " (which he later defines as including education, old age pensions, and unemployment insurance) . . . " taxation is a process to which we must all submit gladly." [2] For, he continues, all the objects upon which the revenue is to be spent will, if achieved, with the one exception of the defence of the national honour, " literally pay us." [3]

Perhaps the main cause of this change in outlook is a consciousness that with the rapid development of the industrial revolution, with the progressive division of labour and the greater localization of industry, with specialization extending on an ever-increasing scale from industrial and commercial to financial and agricultural undertakings of all kinds, the social environment has become a common one in a new and unprecedented sense. Men have much larger forces at their disposal, both economic and scientific, than

[1] *Social Statics*, Final Ed., p. 69.
[2] *Our Money and the State*, by Hartley Withers, pp. 6–7. Also p. 24. [3] Ib.

ever before in the history of the world, and private monopoly is pushed to limits previously unknown. As a result, the consequences of the selfish misuse of these forces, whether monopolistic or not, have become more dangerous, or at least more menacing to society, than has hitherto been the case. This condition has indicated the necessity for a more extensive collective control of the environment, and has led to a definite turning away from the uncontrolled economic individualism of the Victorian era. The economists have swung round in a far more startling fashion than is realized by the average citizen, who generally imagines that the exponents of economic science still promulgate the same kind of individualistic doctrine as their predecessors in the classical days of Adam Smith and his disciples. Yet this is far from being the case. " It is as idle to expect a well-planned town to result from the independent activities of isolated speculators," says Professor Pigou, " as it would be to expect a satisfactory picture to result if each separate square inch were painted by an independent artist. No ' invisible hand ' can be relied on to produce a good arrangement of the whole from a combination of separate treatment of the parts. It is, therefore, necessary that an authority of wider powers should intervene and should tackle the collective problems of beauty, of air and of light." [1]   Dr. Marshall follows the

[1] *Economics of Welfare*, by A. C. Pigou, pp. 170-1.

same line of thought when he says that " a closely peopled district is impoverished by every one who adds a new building or raises an old one higher. . . . For the sake of a little material wealth we are wasting those energies which are the factors of production of all wealth." [1] The most important development in the modern world is the growth of various forms of conscious control, actual or attempted, by man over the conditions of his existence. The same tendency is visible whether we turn to physical science, or psychological research, or biology, or birth control, or town planning. The opinion of the foremost economists lends weight to the suggestion that much more attention should be paid to the conscious control by the community of the social and economic environment.

It may perhaps be said that, in proving that private income is of very little avail as regards certain elements, we have proved too much. For if private income is as unavailing for obtaining certain of the essential forms of welfare as I have made it out to be, why trouble about its distribution at all ? Inequalities of income may exist, my questioner might continue ; but they are not accompanied by consequential inequalities of welfare in many essential matters. The reply to this is obvious. It is true that increases of income bring the individual no return, or almost no

[1] *Principles of Economics*, by A. Marshall, p 659.

return, so far as certain of the elements of welfare are concerned. But it is just for that reason that the enormous inequalities of income which at present exist are so disadvantageous. For while the possessors of even the largest private incomes do not acquire thereby the means with which to attain to a state of well-being in regard to many elements of the good life, the collective effort which would effectively increase those elements cannot be made so long as so much income remains in private hands for consumption in ways which are wasteful in so far as they do not result in welfare either to the wealthy possessors or to others. Obviously the larger the share of income that is left in private hands the less there is available in proportion for public expenditure. We must be careful, of course, to distinguish in this connexion between proportions or shares of income and aggregate amounts. For example, the portion of a private income going to the public revenue in various ways for purposes of collective expenditure might increase in absolute amount although the proportion which that portion bore to the total private income of the individual might have diminished. Similarly the share of the total going to public purposes might increase while the aggregate amount diminished.

It appears likely that in modern developed industrial societies the financial needs of public activity increase, even as regards existing services, in relation to the total amount of the national dividend. Thus it is no answer to the argument which I have herein-before advanced to say that the sum total of private income available for public expenditure has increased very largely during the past century. The question of its relation to the national income must also be considered ; and even that does not carry the matter very far.

Another of the main conclusions which emerges from this investigation is that if we wish to obtain clear ideas concerning economic and social welfare, it is necessary for us to think less in terms of money values generally, and money income in particular, and more in terms of the various elements of welfare, and the way in which they affect the lives of individual men and women. The "measuring rod of money" is quite inadequate to express much what is connected with these elements ; and we shall do better to think, quantitatively so far as possible, in terms of the elements themselves. The distinction between the two methods of thought is vividly brought out, despite a slight artistic exaggeration of statement, by Professor Patrick Geddes, when he speaks of those who descant about " 'our vast and increasing accumulations of wealth' here in the Bank of England and there in the village Savings Banks ; but to the direct eye of the social surveyor . . . this accumulation of wealth remains after all too much the same : a vision for the most part of growing infinitudes of mean streets, mean houses, mean backyards, relieved more or less by bigger ones, too often even duller still." [1]

It cannot be too strongly emphasized that there is nothing " uneconomic " in regarding wealth in terms of the elements of welfare rather than in terms of money values or money income.   Despite a widely held belief to the contrary by persons unacquainted with the subject, economic science is by no means necessarily wedded to money values, but is, on the almost unanimous showing of its modern exponents, primarily concerned with human welfare and its attainment. The elements of welfare with which we have here dealt are essentially economic in that they have to do with the material conditions of human welfare in the ordinary sense of the term.   It is true that economists are often unjustifiably preoccupied with money values, but this is due to a defect of method rather than to an intention to confine the subject-matter to a narrow channel.

We have, therefore, remained essentially within the economic sphere in pursuing the enquiry which has been made in these pages ; and we have been concerned, not with a change in subject-matter, but with the abandonment of a false calculus. The absurdity of that calculus becomes manifest as soon as we attempt to compare the relative welfare of nations by computing the monetary wealth, either aggregate or average, of

[1] *Cities in Evolution*, p. 69.

their members. The same thing occurs if we take for comparison the state of well-being even of particular individuals living in different countries. We find at once that monetary wealth is a most inadequate index of welfare, since it not only ignores all moral or ethical values in reference to that wealth, but excludes from consideration all manner of things, such as, for example, the æsthetic sense, climatic conditions, social harmony, the intellectual atmosphere, and so forth, which may have but little relation to an ability to afford clothes of the best wool, or to satisfy carnivorous instincts three times a day. As Mr. Graham Wallas has said, " two types of industrial organization might . . . be equally efficient in the production of wealth, and yet life under one might be happy and under another unhappy." [1]

The readjustment of ideas which we have ventured to suggest leads to the conception of income as being that which comes in to the life of the individual in the shape of the various elements of welfare, whether received directly in kind or indirectly through the medium of private wealth, and whether through the agency of private activity and private disbursement or through collective effort and public expenditure. Thus it *may* include not only all the ordinary goods and services of everyday production and exchange ; but also certain human relationships and incorporeal satisfactions of

[1] *The Great Society*, p. 321.

165

various kinds. We come, in short, to evaluate life in terms of life, and income in terms of welfare. This breaks down the absurd illusion that economic welfare consists of, or follows automatically from, certain things or services acquired by an individual, and enables us to get back to the effect which those commodities or services have upon that individual. In this way income becomes subjective rather than objective ; and what would be an increment of income to one man might be the very opposite if it were applied to another.

One result of this conception of income is that it involves a vital change in our ideas concerning incentives to work. Since it is a fact that increases of money income, or of the so-called real income, often fail to bring to the recipient any increases of welfare in some of its most important aspects, it is clear that society cannot continue to rely indefinitely on the actual acquisition of additional increments of money income, or on the expectation of or hope or desire for additional increments, as a sufficient motive to induce men and women to make the vast efforts which are required if the existing economic standard of life is to be maintained. Even if that were possible, the outlook would be a poor one, for it is obvious that if life is to be made tolerable for great masses of human beings in the western countries, the mere maintenance of existing standards is not enough : new creative effort on an unparalleled scale is also needed imperatively.

CONCORD

At present we do actually rely on the desire for a larger income, either in terms of money or of the commodities and services which money can buy, as the main incentive to new effort. But the assumption underlying this desire is not borne out by the facts ; and the economic machine in consequence runs slowly and fitfully and in jerks and starts. Unconsciously, mankind is gradually coming to feel that the identification of income with welfare is illusory ; with the result, as Henry Ford observes, that " to be rich is no longer a common ambition." Yet the motive on which we ostensibly rely, and which we pretend is indispensable to get the work of the world done, and particularly to get new developments started, is precisely the ambition to be rich—or richer. The failure of this ambition to provide a sufficient incentive for the carrying out of activities highly necessary to society can be observed to a greater or lesser extent in every part of the western world. What is happening is something much more deep-rooted and far reaching than a recognition of the mere fact that (in Dr.Cannan's words) " material welfare does not increase *pari passu* with increasing income." [1]

It is obvious that, although income has a diminishing utility—to say the very least, and to put it much lower than I have hereinbefore argued—this cannot be said of welfare itself. I do not assert for a moment that the

[1] *The Economic Outlook*, p. 273.

elements which have been discussed in these pages comprise the sum total of human well-being : such an assumption would be contrary to the whole spirit of the enquiry, the object of which has been to suggest a method of analysis, a way of looking at things, which would help to bridge the gulf which still exists between wealth and welfare. Human welfare comprises an infinitude of complex elements of which no neat list can be made. Freedom, the conditions of marriage and parenthood ; honour, property, and security for the home ; law, love, fraternity and scientific knowledge ; these and a hundred other ingredients of the good life can be distinguished and have each their place ; while behind all, overshadowing all, embracing all, loom the religious beliefs and philosophical conceptions of the human spirit. In the last resort welfare must be considered as a single and indivisible resulting unity, complex and elusive, rather than as a combination of known factors ; and to it may well be applied the remark which Mr. Lytton Strachey has made concerning art : " There is a spark within it which defies foreknowledge." [1]

The peculiar curse of our age is what may be called the Monetary Interpretation of Welfare ; but I think that by shifting our thoughts from income to welfare and its constituent elements we shall be less liable to be embedded in the morass of materialism than when

[1] *Books and Characters*, p. 11.

168

the ordinary methods of valuation in monetary terms are employed as a method of assessing human well-being. The pursuit of wealth, like the use of force, is in itself neither good nor bad ; and whether or not it suffers from materialism depends upon the origin of the wealth, the methods by which it is produced, the manner in which it is employed, and by whom it is used. There is a great deal of truth in Dr. Marshall's words when he says that " so long as wealth is applied to provide for every family the necessities of life and culture, and an abundance of the higher forms of enjoyment for collective use, so long the pursuit of wealth is a noble aim." [1] It is when the minds of men become preoccupied with the outward forms of wealth, which may or may not produce the " states of consciousness " of which welfare consists, that the pursuit tends to become base and ignoble. It is when the souls of men are dominated by mere things, and wealth is regarded as something objective and unconditional rather than as subjective and qualified, that materialism corrodes the heart of society and turns the world into a wilderness of strife and misery. It is, in short, the general identification of wealth with welfare, and in particular the confusion of private wealth not only with the common good but also with the welfare of the owner thereof, that leads men to waste their substance in a vain and rapacious scramble for the

[1] *Principles of Economics,* p. 137.

power to acquire possessions and command services that bring satisfaction neither to themselves nor to others, but which nevertheless deprive whole hosts of their fellow creatures of true forms of well-being.

To think of wealth in terms of welfare and its elements should help us to avoid the abstractness which is the main cause of materialism in the modern world. It is possible, and, indeed, our common practice, to think of ships and shoes and sealing wax, and the monetary value of such commodities, in an entirely abstract manner without in the least considering their physical or psychological effect upon the lives of human beings. But the elements of welfare are essentially subjective, for they are nothing save the attributes of human beings. Thus discussion or reflection concerning health, or æsthetic experience, or the acquisition of knowledge, postulates, nay, demands in the mind of the thinker an awareness of the existence of men and women, the contemplation of whose physical or mental condition forms part of the very subject-matter itself. This in turn may lead to what Mr. James Harvey Robinson calls " the easily demonstrated scientific truth that nearly all men and women, whatever their social and economic status, may have much greater possibilities of activity and thought and emotion than they exhibit in the particular conditions in which they happen to be placed " ; [1] that everywhere

[1] *The Mind in the Making*, p. 166.

is to be found evidence of unrealized capacity ; that the whole plane of our existence is on a lower scale than is necessary with the human material and the knowledge and power at our disposal.

Great biological and psychological difficulties will have to be overcome if we are to acquire the mental habit of thinking continuously of material well-being in terms of the non-monetary individual welfare, actual and potential, of large numbers of men and women and children ; and no one who has seriously observed the effects of our modern large-scale civilization upon human dispositions and instincts will be inclined to underrate the obstacles which will be encountered. But unless they are overcome I do not believe that any real economic or social progress is likely to be made. If we did in fact secure that change much else that may seem superficially more important would follow almost automatically ; and the human race might go forward to its destiny in a way which no man can foretell in sober language.

INDEX

172

INDEX

INDEX

PRINTED BY UNWIN BROTHERS, LIMITED, LONDON AND WOKING, GREAT BRITAIN

Printed in the United States
by Baker & Taylor Publisher Services